EARLY CHILDHOOD EDUCATION SERIES
Leslie R. Williams, Editor

ADVISORY BOARD: Barbara T. Bowman, Harriet K. Cuffaro,
Stephanie Feeney, Doris Pronin Fromberg, Celia Genishi, Stacie G. Goffin,
Dominic F. Gullo, Alice Sterling Honig, Elizabeth Jones, Gwen Morgan

(Continued)

Negotiating Standards in the Primary Classroom

THE TEACHER'S DILEMMA

CAROL ANNE WIEN

Foreword by Lilian G. Katz

Teachers College, Columbia University
New York and London

Chapter 2 is an expanded version of Carol Anne Wien's article, "Coping with Standardized Curriculum in Kindergarten: Portrait of an Exemplary Early Childhood Educator," *Early Childhood Education*, Vol. 35 (Spring/Summer, 2002), pp. 14–21. Used by permission of the Alberta Teachers' Association.

Chapter 3 is a slightly adapted version of Carol Anne Wien's article "The Press of Standardized Curriculum: Does a Kindergarten Teacher Instruct with Worksheets or Let Children Play?," *Canadian Children*, Vol. 27 (2002), pp. 10–17. Used with permission of the Journal of Canadian Association for Young Children.

Chapter 8 is an expanded version of Carol Anne Wien's article, "Portrait of a Teacher Using Science to Integrate Curriculum," *Early Childhood Education*, Vol. 35 (Spring/Summer, 2002), pp. 33–42. Used by permission of the Alberta Teachers' Association.

Published by Teachers College Press, 1234 Amsterdam Avenue, New York, NY 10027

Library of Congress Cataloging-in-Publication Data

Wien, Carol Anne, 1944–
    Negotiating standards in the primary classroom : the teacher's dilemma / Carol Anne Wien ; foreword by Lilian Katz.
        p. cm. — (Early childhood education series)
    Includes bibliographical references and index.
    ISBN 0-8077-4511-1 (cloth : alk. paper) — ISBN 0-8077-4510-3 (pbk. : alk. paper)
        1. Early childhood education—Standards—Canada—Toronto—Case studies.   2. Early childhood education—Canada—Toronto—Case studies.   I. Title.   II. Early childhood education series (Teachers College Press)
    LB1139.3.C2W54 2004
    372.21'09713'541—dc22   2004051732

ISBN 0-8077-4510-3 (paper)
ISBN 0-8077-4511-1 (cloth)

Printed on acid-free paper
Manufactured in the United States of America

11   10   09   08   07   06   05   04   8   7   6   5   4   3   2   1

To my mother, Georgie Matthews,
for a lifetime's beauty, music, loving support,
and spirited engagement with the world

Contents

Foreword

Contemporary education in North America is marked by intense pressure on teachers of all age groups to produce predetermined standardized effects on those that they teach. Terms like program standards, learning standards, content standards, academic and achievement standards, benchmarks, indicators, and performance outcomes—typically set at the state level—mark much of the discussion among teachers at all levels of education today. In this book, Carol Anne Wien engages us in a close look at how eight teachers—working in the public schools of metropolitan Toronto, Canada—dealt with an imposed standardized curriculum and its associated assessment requirements.

While efforts to meet official standards for content and skill learning in the upper elementary and secondary grades generate great pressure on teachers and their pupils, they are even more likely to produce conflict and distress for teachers of our youngest children. Long lists of pre-specified outcomes, referred to in this study as "expectations," are clearly at odds with the strong tradition of developmentally appropriate and child-sensitive pedagogical and curriculum practices in early childhood education. This book gives us an intimate look at how eight teachers of young children struggled to cope with the exacting standards imposed upon them. The sheer number of expectations required by the standardized curriculum is mind-numbing. For example, in first grade, the Science and Technology section of the standardized curriculum consisted of three "overall expectations"—20 specific expectations for each of five strands. In this way, the science curriculum alone consisted of about 100 expectations for outcomes. When all of the content strands are combined, teachers are attempting to achieve more than 500 expectations for any given grade level.

In addition to the sheer number of expectations, teachers had to wrestle with the fact that, while some of the expectations were specific, and others were very vague—all of which contributed to complex issues concerning the management of time. As Wien points out, the teachers often felt that they were being forced into a factory production-schedule-model of time organization that would likely undermine the chances of success for many children. In addition, each child was to be regularly assessed on every expectation. As the author shares her discussions with the teachers, we begin to understand their predicament. Not only did these demands take a great deal of the satisfaction out of teaching, teachers also worried that the children's joy in learning was threatened by the industrialization of their classroom life.

Wien addresses the fundamental question of whether good early childhood education can exist in schools that are obliged to follow a standardized curriculum with hundreds of required outcomes. All of the teachers shared their frustrations concerning the requirement to prepare reports of each child's progress at specific levels of learning, considering such assessments to be both difficult as well as risky to apply in the early years of schooling. Teachers had to devote much time to gathering evidence for assigning letter grades on report cards—each grade meant to represent what a child had achieved on dozens of expectations. Similarly, we also see one of the major pitfalls of such a highly segmented curriculum: Teachers are under pressure to proceed on to the next fragment of the curriculum, whether or not all of the children in the class have fully grasped the information and concepts to be mastered. What if the teacher realizes some time after teaching a particular concept that some of the children have not quite mastered it, are confused about it, or have forgotten it? Due to serious time constraints, the teacher could not return to the topic to clear up remaining confusion among some of the children.

A standardized curriculum that is accompanied by so many formal rubrics by which to assess its achievement for each child is difficult enough when the children are older. However, Wien helps us to see that, during the earliest years of schooling, these practices make the developmental appropriateness of the curriculum and associated teaching methods almost—but not entirely—impossible. Everyday these teachers' lives present them with a major dilemma: Should they focus on satisfying the detailed requirements of the standardized curriculum and risk forfeiting many important aspects of the children's developmental needs? Or should they focus primarily on the children's needs and risk failing to satisfy the regulations that govern their employment? Such is the nature of a dilemma: Addressing one of its two horns means neglecting the potential benefits of addressing the other.

Wien takes us with her into the classrooms of the eight teachers as they devote themselves to addressing the standards, to being responsive to the developmental nature of their students, and to addressing the challenging diversity of the children in their classes. We can see, up close, how the teachers experienced feelings of being overwhelmed and stressed as they attempted a variety of strategies by which to do justice to the hundreds of specific expectations of the standardized curriculum and to the normal attributes of kindergarten and primary-level learners.

All of the teachers tried to deal with their conviction that young children benefit most from meaningful, direct, and first-hand experiences, rather than the kind of rote learning that the large number of expectations and time constraints seemed to make necessary. Wien puts the conflicts in the context of developmentally appropriate practice versus mechanistic methods based on an industrial or factory approach to education. The vivid observations shared in this book present an interesting variety of ways teachers can adapt to the constraints and demands of the curriculum. Some of them were willing, although reluctantly, to take the curriculum as a prescription for a series of time-bound lessons. Others managed to develop an integrated and holistic way to respond to it.

The eight teachers are sufficiently diverse in their backgrounds, training, and experience that most teachers will be able to identify with one or two of them. The rich descriptions of the contexts in which the teachers struggle can help readers imagine and reflect upon how they themselves might respond to similar situations. These teachers also work in a variety of physical conditions, combined classes, and team-teaching arrangements that help readers to gain insight into various ways of addressing the complexities of the demands placed on those who let us into their classrooms. These teachers also offer examples of how best to ensure that the curriculum is meaningful to young children of different cultural, ethnic, and language backgrounds, as well as to those with a variety of special needs.

Wien helps us to appreciate how the teachers' experience and training influenced their choices of how best to deal with the complex demands placed on them. On the basis of her observations and discussions with each teacher, Wien strongly recommends allocating resources for professional development to help teachers cope with this trend in education. We are also alerted to how principals' preferences and attitudes affect teachers' abilities to cope with the predicaments created by the standards and the rubrics. The author makes the point that a teacher's relationship with her colleagues can, for better or worse, play an important role in situations like those described.

At the close of each of the chapters, Wien summarizes the constraints, choices, and possibilities that she observes, helping us to put her observations into a fuller context. The variety of strategies teachers use provide a rich source of ideas about what to try. The stories of the eight teachers present an amazing range of what works, what's best for children, and what helps them the most.

Wien shares rich insights concerning the various risks to students presented by each of the different teacher's adaptations to the curriculum. She also raises some difficult questions for us to ponder. For example, is it possible that when teachers are obliged to work in 15-minute segments of time in order to cover so many expectations, constantly stopping and starting children on each set of tasks in turn, we are teaching the children that what they are learning or doing doesn't really matter much, anyway? Can such a "piece work" style of teaching support the development, expression, and strengthening of important intellectual dispositions? Such questions, and many others raised here, deserve serious discussion among all of us concerned with early education. Wien offers us an opportunity to look closely at possible answers to many important questions, and shares her view of the implications of the troubling trend toward the fragmentation and mechanization of education.

Although the teachers and classrooms so thoughtfully described in this book were in an area north of the U.S. border, their stories support the view that teachers who work with young children have much in common with their peers in other countries.

—Lilian G. Katz

Preface

This book investigates how early childhood teachers are responding to the political demands of teaching standardized curriculum in public school classrooms, kindergarten through second grade. How do teachers who believe in developmentally appropriate practice and a complex, responsive, child-centered practice cope with the imposition of standardized curricula and reporting systems? What do these mean to them, and how do they work with them, given the legal requirement that they do so, particularly if their belief system tells them this is intellectually and pedagogically unsound for young children?

I began the research upon which this book is based thinking that case studies of 6 to 10 teachers would offer helpful portraits showing a range of examples of what is happening in elementary schools. I worked with five teachers in 1999–2000 and three more in 2000–2001. I recognized that not all elementary teachers of kindergarten through second grade start from a position of valuing or necessarily understanding developmentally appropriate practice, and I hoped to convince several teachers of more traditional persuasion to participate in order to investigate their views of the changes and the impact on their teaching practice. There are many versions of child-centered approaches, accomplished through whole-language programs, inquiry-based programs, brain-based education, or multiple intelligences approaches, as well as many versions of traditional teaching. As you engage with the teachers portrayed here, you will make your own interpretation of where teachers are located in terms of frameworks for practice, ranging from child-centered to traditional.

The mission I set myself was to act as an honest witness investigating the conditions under which teachers of young children teach. My intent was to acknowledge and clarify the complexity of teachers' teaching lives, illustrating what goes into their thinking, the actions they take, their views of what they are doing, and how the children in their classrooms respond. While I appreciate those who use the wide-angle lens and bring us broad understandings via quantitative measures, my own way inevitably is to focus intently, as through a microscope, on a few individual contexts to see what they tell us about larger issues.

This book creates portraits of eight public school teachers working in their early childhood classrooms in a large metropolitan area in Canada. It shows these teachers taking up the standardized curriculum of the Conservative government in Ontario at the time, how they make it work in their own classroom, their struggles with it, the stresses and challenges that it imposes, and the constructive solutions that they have invented or found to meet those challenges. It shows places where they are stumped, where they have confronted problems and created solutions, and where the problems are as yet unresolved or even unseen. The book documents a range of approaches to the standardized curriculum, and questions whether a standardized curriculum ever in fact can work in the way intended by policy levels.

Standards surround us in every field of endeavor. The press of government regulating bodies in attempting to guarantee specific levels of quality is understandable, as a way of demonstrating to taxpayers the soundness of a government's governing. Simultaneously, where living systems are concerned—humans, animals, plants, and ecosystems—there is the pressing question of whether prescriptive approaches that "implement" standards can achieve what they set out to. This is so simply because humans are responsive agents and, through their participation, affect what happens. While the early childhood field does not ignore standardized curricula and testing (Kohn, 2001; Wesson, 2001), the impetus of the field is to begin with children, not curriculum, and to be responsive to families so that power is shared. I began this investigation wondering whether the policy sphere exerts—because of its legal force—so much power over children, teachers, and administrators in schools that this power overrides the deep theoretical, practical, and historical knowledge of the field of early childhood education for those teachers who bring this background to schools. I wanted to see whether early childhood education could exist as part of schools coping with standards.

What I hope to do in the book is invite readers into a conversation about a big issue—how teachers in early childhood negotiate standardized curriculum—as a way of deepening our understanding of learning, teaching, schools, and the nature of teachers' work. But so that you can make your own judgments about my interpretations of teaching, I offer my perspective, as suggested by Lawrence-Lightfoot and Hoffman-Davis (1997) in their description of portraiture as both science and art.

THE RESEARCHER'S PERSPECTIVE

When I enter the classrooms of early elementary teachers, I do so with my own background coloring my interpretations. There were but three work choices for a young woman when I graduated from high school in the 1960s—to become a secretary, nurse, or teacher. I first taught high school in Ontario, and then fell into the education reform movement of the late 1960s by becoming a Montessori preschool teacher in Ithaca, New York. At the time it seemed really radical. As a Montessori teacher I learned nontraditional structures for organizing time and space in classrooms: for instance, I learned how to organize space so that 25 children could be doing different things simultaneously. After 7 years I left Montessori teaching for graduate work, to sort out my concern about children's play (which Montessori thought a "distortion" of reality) and my hunch that its imaginative, symbolic aspect was critical to children's development. I have studied and worked in university settings ever since. My thinking about standardized curriculum is colored, too, by the fact that I was taught under the sway of such a curriculum in the 1950s. I remember that it was often boring, and took a long time to get to do anything: we just got started and the teacher told us it was time to do something else. Yet as I watch teachers, I am astonished at how interesting they can make an abstract concept by connecting it to children's lives, and have seen some of them make amazing things happen for children under difficult circumstances. I see the purpose of my work largely as the support of teachers of young children.

In addition, since 1989 I have been deeply affected by the Reggio Emilia Approach (originating in the city of Reggio Emilia, Italy). I am intrigued by its comprehensive congruence of philosophy, values, and actual practice; inspired by the hope it creates for the successful construction of places of active co-participation in democratic processes that build a "civil society"; and delighted by its emphasis on multiple modes of knowing and representation of knowledge. I cannot help but look at teaching now with that powerful exemplar from another language and culture affecting my interpretation of what we might try to make in our own conflicted culture. So my understanding of Montessori, of child development and developmentally appropriate practice (Wien, 1995), and of Reggio Emilia, and my adult life as a professor of early childhood education provide a counterpoint both to my childhood experience and to my adult knowledge of schools as places of standardized curriculum.

The language of government documents is dry and abstract: abstractions are outlines and omit experience—all the lived life of teaching and learning. To become absorbed by standardized curricula with rigid levels, rubrics, tests, and measurements is a dislocating way to live. Are teachers able to find meaning in their work, to find relevance to children's lives and love of the world and its ecological diversity, beauty, pattern, and texture? How do teachers sustain themselves through mechanistic, competitive, production-driven processes? Teachers and children are replete with soul, with energy for living. Are they able to embed the abstract in rich class-room lives and so liberate themselves and the children they teach?

ACKNOWLEDGMENTS

I feel a strong sense of loyalty to the teachers who so graciously opened their classrooms and their hearts to me and hope I have done them justice. They work so hard and they care so much. They astonish me for their grace under pressure, their determined sprightliness, the way they construct joy in the face of overwhelming demands. Teaching is not stable, yet they must create stable worlds for the children in their care. I would also like to thank the school board for permission to enter its domain.

My thanks and appreciation to the teachers of the York University Early Childhood Education Series 2003–2004 for inviting their children to provide illustrations, and my special thanks to the children for their vibrant drawings.

Graduate students Sara Furnival and later Ainsley Brown transcribed taped interviews with aplomb and assisted in other ways that I appreciated. Ainsley danced around the technology with infectious delight. Both had the capacity to get things done with speed and accuracy.

I am grateful to many colleagues but mention here in particular Ann Manicom, Deborah Britzman, Louise Cadwell, Lous Heshusius, Randa Khattar, and Sharon Murphy. Stacie Goffin was generous in offering support in understanding the standards movement in the United States, as was Curt Dudley-Marling. In the early stages of the book, Elizabeth Jones and Pacific Oaks College welcomed me as a Visiting Scholar, and I thank them for their hospitality and for collegial discussions.

I am very grateful to Lilian Katz for providing the foreword: Her perspicacity, incisive comments, and compelling vision have provided leadership to use for a long time and continue to inspire us. Leslie Williams, series editor of renown, has done such good work for so long and the early childhood field is enormously indebted to her. I thank her, with tenderness and hope for her future, for her supportive suggestions regarding the orchestration of this book. And Susan Liddicoat works with such patience and gracious persistence, and is astonishing in being able to see with clarity both the macro and micro levels of text.

My parents, Georgie and Joe Matthews, my children, Erika and Otis Wien, and my husband, Fred Wien, offer the support and stability of a loving family, the foundation of all my work, and my gratitude is boundless.

CHAPTER 1

Early Childhood Teachers in Public Schools

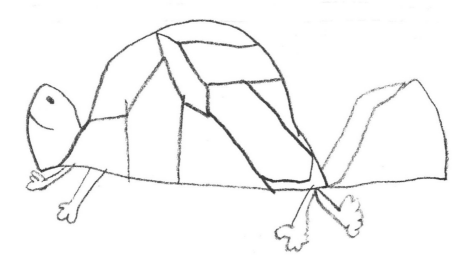

Teachers of young children in public schools struggle with the tension of being pulled between contradictory frameworks for teaching. On the one hand, these teachers recognize that to be pedagogically sound they must offer children real experience of the world, active learning, and freedom to explore and play. Such opportunities provide children with complex opportunities for planning, organizing, and interpreting their experience, for engaging with others, for initiating ideas, and for negotiating friendships and attachments to the world. By whatever name one prefers to give it, teachers in early childhood education believe that children learn best through play-based, child-centered, developmentally appropriate programs in which experiences are personally meaningful to the children (Bredekamp & Copple, 1997). On the other hand, in public schools there has been increasing pressure over the past 20 years at policy levels to increase academic training in class-rooms for young children (Allen, 2001; Elkind, 1990).

The standards movement—the development by governments of stan-dards for many arenas of functioning in society—has swept westernized nations over the past 15 years (McRel Web site www.mcrel.org; British Web site www.dfes.gov.uk). In education, standards were developed for all sub-ject areas by the mid-1990s, defended by a mechanistic rationale that sees education like constructing a machine: "Americans . . . expect strict stan-dards to govern construction of buildings, bridges, highways, and tunnels . . . Standards are created because they improve the activity of life" (Ravitch, 1995, pp. 8–9 in McRel Web site). This book asks whether standards im-prove the lives of teachers and children. Standards in education are descriptions of what learners "should" be able to do and "should" know at specific points in their education. Standardized testing has increasingly been used as the means by which to judge whether the standard has been reached. A standardized curriculum is a one-size-fits-all program of spe-cific content to be learned; it is used as the instrument by which a set of standards "will" be reached.

The standards movement reaches into early childhood education on two fronts. One is the sets of Early Learning Outcomes established for child care programs. The other is the various standardized curricula developed by states, school boards, and commercial publishing companies that apply to kindergarten through third grade. This book is concerned with the con-text of schools, and with the education of children kindergarten through second grade. Is there a trend in the United States and Canada toward stan-dardized curriculum in kindergarten through third grade in schools? Yes. By 1999, all states but Iowa had adopted standards in education (McRel Web site), and by 2003 in Canada, so had most provinces (Council of Min-isters of Education, personal communication, March 22, 2004). Another example of standardization is the presence of basal reading programs (com-mercially published) in 80% of states (Dudley-Marling, personal conver-sation, January 2004).

We cannot fault policy levels for trying to describe what a society wants to achieve, and for trying to decide if in fact that achievement has occurred. Indeed, the standardized curriculum represented in this study, when I read it through, seemed direct and simple, a set of descriptions that could raise few objections. Yet there is little in the reality it creates for teachers that is simple, direct, and unproblematic. Early childhood education has always had a tenuous toehold in kindergarten through third grade because it con-tradicts conventional schooling in its beliefs and pedagogies. Can early childhood education exist in schools with standardized curriculum? This book addresses that question.

When teachers work in the early childhood years, there are four areas of concern that they must integrate in every teaching decision:

1. Developmental knowledge of young children.
2. Understanding the interests, capacities, and needs of the specific children in their classroom.
3. Knowledge of the sociocultural background of these children and their families (and all related equity issues around language, culture, class, race, and gender).
4. Knowledge of curriculum and pedagogical strategies (what to teach and how) (Bredekamp & Copple, 1997; Bredekamp & Rosegrant, 1992, 1995).

The documents describing these aspects of teaching young children (such as those cited above) are highly regarded in the field of early childhood education as attempts to define complex practice, are studied in Early Childhood Education programs, and are practiced directly in field placements. These four areas of concern must be thought through and balanced in every decision in teaching practice. Teachers who coordinate these four sets of reference points as they make moment-to-moment decisions about practice are engaged in a highly sophisticated, complex balancing act that should not be underestimated by those who do not work with young children.

As a teacher educator, I began the research that underpins this book because I wanted to know how public school teachers of young children were taking up a standardized curriculum when it suggested working in ways that might be opposite to their beliefs, values, and previous practice. In what range of ways were teachers approaching this difficult challenge? Did they think their teaching had changed, and if so, how? I hypothesized that I might see two patterns. On the one hand, I expected to find some teachers had given up on developmentally appropriate practice or child-centered approaches, because I was seeing and hearing about returns to rows of desks, individual work, worksheets, an emphasis on drill, rote memory, and an academic stance with young children. I also hypothesized that I would find some continuation of the more open-ended stance toward teaching young children among highly experienced teachers, and wondered how they were doing it. Thus the questions with which I began can be summarized as follows:

- What are the different ways teachers in kindergarten through second grade are taking up the standardized curriculum?
- How do they think their teaching has changed as a consequence of the standardized curriculum?

- What compels teachers to take up the standardized curriculum in linear, lockstep ways, reducing education to worksheets, workbooks, and attempts to "cover" curriculum with young children?
- What permits teachers to sustain developmentally appropriate practices, or child-centered and play-based approaches, and continue to work competently with the standardized curriculum?
- What other approaches are evident?

Why does it matter to understand teachers' practice with a standardized curriculum? It matters as one way of showing policymakers the consequences of actions taken at the macro level. This book helps to make visible to policymakers, administrators, and curriculum specialists examples of the consequences of their decisions for the daily lives of teachers and children. Policy levels emphasize test scores, and this study shows experiential data omitted from testing: these "real-world" results are as important as test scores.

This study is also important as a forum for experienced teachers within which they may compare their own experience and understand that their situation is systemic, not individual. It is, in addition, extremely useful to have such information as this research provides when thinking about teacher preparation, and in particular how to support new teachers in sustaining developmentally appropriate practice in contexts of standardized curriculum.

THE CONTEXT

Toronto, the metropolitan region in Ontario, Canada, in which this research occurred, is an interesting example of the general situation. A Conservative government for the province of Ontario that was elected in 1995 introduced a standardized curriculum in 1997 built around the notion of clear, observable expectations or outcomes. Teachers and school personnel were granted 3 years to "implement" the curriculum, in other words, to learn these expectations and work out how to assist children in reaching them. Introduced alongside this new curriculum was a report card with grades of A, B, C, and D "leveled" to specific selected expectations. The imposition of this standardized curriculum and standardized reporting system was tumultuous and sudden and followed a period of roughly 30 years of much more open curriculum, left to the determination of each school board. But there had been complaints from workplaces, universities, parents, and media for 10 to 15 years that the open system was too varied, that graduates were too illiterate and innumerate, that the system was not sufficiently rigorous (Lewington &

Orpwood, 1993). Coupled with these concerns was the ever-present worry that in the climate of globalization, the metropolitan region, which is the economic engine of a large geographical area and produces 20% of the GNP for the entire country, would not be able to compete, and would lose out in terms of economic power.

The focal point of the region is Toronto, with a population of two million, bordering a lake. Behind and around the city, in a rainbow shape, lies suburban sprawl and a further three to four million people (depending where you stop counting), crowding in on older towns and villages. In the past 35 years this urban area has spread like a wandering amoeba. At its outer edges farmland becomes suburbs in a mere two months: drive by any field in this range and know it won't be corn or wheat for long. The 16-lane major highway across the top of the city is clogged by 7:30 in the morning. I mentioned a lake: it is very far away, separated from the city by a huge raised throughway carrying traffic across the lower end of the city from east to west. The lake has little impact on the life of the city, its shoreline unsuitable for recreation and overtaken a century ago by industry.

Since 1965 immigrants have arrived in the city and suburbs by the hundreds of thousands, a steady flow from everywhere in the world. School life has changed. Principals in some areas say they know, watching the news and the most recent outbreaks of war, whose children will be showing up shortly in their schools. In this respect, the city is like all other major centers in the Western world, a recipient of massive cultural migrations. These cultural groups new to the city and its culture in the past generation are interwoven through many areas of the city, with knots of culture forming neighborhoods such as a Greek area, Chinatown, a Portuguese area, a Korean area. There are areas where people settle upon arrival, and move on from once established. Further out in the suburbs, high-rise apartment buildings are known as centers of Somali immigrants, of Ghanese immigrants, or the multiple cultures of India and southeast Asia—Gujarat, Punjabi, Sri Lankan, Vietnamese. There are many new schools in the suburban areas. Schools project enrollments in part on the number of houses being built in an area: one vice principal told me that on the first day of school, three times the number of expected children enrolled, all dropped off in cars by their parents, so that the entrance felt like an airport.

In Canada, education is controlled by the provincial governments and public schools are operated by school boards, a collection of schools organized by geographical proximity. School boards are thus roughly comparable to school districts in the United States. When I refer to a school board, think of a school district. In Ontario, the Conservative government of the time took over direct control of education and removed many school board personnel, who were seconded to the Ministry of Education and Training.

School board directors complained that phone calls to the ministry simply were not returned. Thus while the standardized curriculum was mandated, it was left up to individual boards to implement this curriculum.

Thus in September 1997, elementary teachers suddenly faced a new curriculum, with hundreds of separate expectations for each grade, which landed on their doorstep just as school began. There was little or no in-service preparation for teachers. In addition, there were other serious stressors in the general context surrounding teaching. The provincial government introduced new funding formulas for education that resulted in massive cutbacks in the hundreds of millions of dollars for school boards: consequences included the removal of many curriculum consultants, audiovisual and resource personnel, lunch monitors, and other support services to schools. Teachers in the area are members of strong unions: there have been numerous and frequent job actions, work-to-rule situations, and outright strikes—sometimes two or three per year—which have added enormously to the climate of disruption and chaos in teaching. In the face of these massive changes and difficulties, experienced teachers retired by the thousands. Schools faced shortages of teachers and particularly of substitute teachers, with teachers having to double up classes. The remaining teachers have been left in a highly vulnerable position: they must implement a new standardized curriculum and report card system with reduced resources and minimal support in the midst of continuing disruption.

THE STANDARDIZED CURRICULUM AND REPORTING SYSTEM

The government introduced a standardized curriculum and reporting system in 1997–99 to be more accountable to parents and other electors, to smooth out differences in educational standards across its jurisdiction, and to raise the standards of the system to a more rigorous level. The Ministry of Education and Training published the curriculum separated into subject areas and published documents on Science and Technology, The Arts, Mathematics, Language Arts, and Social Studies (for grades 1–6). The Kindergarten Program was published separately. The Mathematics document, based on "new" and language-based math, included themes and processes (such as transformational geometry) that many teachers had never experienced. The Science curriculum was far heftier and more rigorous than its predecessor, and the Arts curriculum was new in its entirety. These documents were introduced as they were completed, the elementary ones between the summer of 1997 and June 1998 (Ministry of Education and Training, 1997, 1998).

This particular standardized curriculum attempts to describe explicitly the *content* to be mastered in school but does not specify *how* learning will occur: thus, it leaves teachers and administrators free to determine specific pedagogies for teaching and learning. Each subject area curriculum offers a general introduction followed by "overall expectations" and "specific expectations" for each of three to five domains (called "strands") within a discipline. For example, in first grade, there are approximately 3 overall and 20 specific expectations for each of 5 strands in the Science and Technology curriculum, thus the science curriculum alone has about 100 expectations. These five strands, or domains of knowledge, are Life Systems, Matter and Materials, Energy and Control, Structures and Mechanisms, and Earth and Space Systems. The expectations are described in terms of observable verbs, such as *identify, describe, design, formulate,* and so forth, and tend to "cover" the basic concepts of a discipline.

While no single expectation is particularly troublesome at the early elementary level, there was, from anecdotal reports, something about the cumulative effect of the set of documents that suggested that teachers felt both overwhelmed and required to focus on the technical at the expense of meaning.

Alongside the standardized curriculum, the term *rubric* suddenly emerged. So what's a rubric? I was perplexed when the term appeared and at first interpreted it to be a synonym for criteria. I found that the word derived from Middle English for *red ocher*, and came to mean the red part of old manuscript titles, like a subtitle, which explains the topic more explicitly. Over time, it came to express the idea of a standard, a set of explicit rules.

It was the connection between rubrics and report cards that appeared most troublesome for teachers in informal conversations, especially early childhood teachers. The report card required a grade of A, B, C, or D on the specific expectation for each subject area, with A referring to a superb level beyond grade level, B referring to mastery, C to occasional but not consistent attainment or attainment with support, and D to sporadic or missed attainment. Many times I heard teachers say they could not bear to give a child in first grade a D.

Through the construction of rubrics referring to observable, measurable outcomes, teachers were to acquire evidence for their judgments of A, B, C, or D. In other words, in this system, the rubric is used as a means of *classifying* children's work according to four levels. This evidence is generally seen to take the form of a piece of written work. One teacher told me:

> It makes me weep. I feel I'm drowning in paper. It's incredibly overwhelmingly time-consuming in terms of paper. I'm wondering how I'm ever going to get all this stuff I've got now in heaps and piles, folders and files, in there

in the right place. Checked off. I've got to do it for every child, for every criterion. (Wien & Dudley-Marling, 1998, p. 411)

That teacher thought she had about 750 performance criteria, with each to be documented with three pieces of paper. I wondered whether teachers' pedagogy was being changed by the requirements for the new reporting system, even when the curriculum itself did not specify *how* teaching was to occur. Would the reporting system itself constrain teachers' teaching so that early childhood processes would become less probable?

EIGHT TEACHERS IN PRIMARY SETTINGS

In this book, we visit schools in one school board. The school jurisdiction is immense, encompassing rural domains to the north, tracts of suburban housing and malls in the middle, and older villages closer to the lake. Many streets, houses, and indeed even the schools all look the same. The brick schools are long and low, often with a clutch of portables out back and bus lanes in front. There are a few small trees and shrubs, and a playgound stretching off in concrete and asphalt. I go in the front doors of these schools: all other doors are locked. Wide hallways, glass walls of doors, polished linoleum corridors, an office with a high counter, a secretary too busy to look up, a sign-in book to log my arrival. Sometimes there is a "Visitor" pin to wear prominently on my jacket. This is the feel of the landscape.

In several schools there is a metal rack standing in the hallway, a stylized tree form sporting miniature flags dangling from its branches that represent the countries from which children in the school have come. Usually there are about 70 flags on a tree. In one school there was a board that said "Welcome" in all the languages spoken by children in the school. While I recognized the Latinate languages and could guess at Norwegian, Swedish, Hungarian, Russian, and so forth, there were 13 languages whose forms I had never seen before, most from the Indian subcontinent— graceful squiggles, unknown spaces around them. The fact of the ESL child's task to leap from such a language to written English stuns me yet again. The government demands a Level 3 (on a scale of 1 to 4, with 4 being above grade level) from schools as a decent level of education: so do real estate firms. The fact that it takes 7 years for children to fully acquire and function intellectually in a second language is not recognized by the government's testing mechanisms.

The school board that agreed to participate in my investigation is recognized for its policy and practices around inclusion of children with special needs, for its response to ESL issues, for its supporting documents that attempt to bridge curriculum requirements and teacher knowledge (e.g., in science), and, during the years of this research, for qualities of strong leadership. The teachers I approached within this board either had been in our B.Ed. undergraduate program requiring an early childhood education (ECE) credential, had participated in an ECE inquiry group, or were suggested by a resource consultant.[1] I knew some professionally, and I didn't know others. There are two kindergarten teachers, and three each for first and second grade. I would like to have included third grade (and it appears here once in a combined second- and third-grade class), but the constraints on my time and the pressure on third-grade teachers from the weeklong May assessment led me to decide it was not advisable.[2] The eight teachers in this book were teaching in six different schools: two were team-teaching, and in another case, two teachers happened by chance to be in the same school.

I know that teachers who agree to open their doors to a researcher are a special group. They are not the stressed-out, burned-out teachers but teachers who know they can make something fine in difficult times, teachers who have enough confidence in their work not to be threatened by an outsider. Before you meet them, we know they are all strong, confident risk-takers. Their names, of course, are pseudonyms (for a description of the research methodology, see Appendix A).

The conversation we are beginning with the teacher-participants asks them how they are taking up the standardized curriculum, how they are finding it works for them, how they wish to work, and how they are in fact working. What are the conditions of their teaching lives? What constraints and possibilities for practice do they see? What choices or "degrees of freedom" do they think they have, and how do they make use of those? What leads them to a particular set of responses to a situation? There are some interesting discussion questions to consider in thinking through their responses (see Appendix B). As we follow them, can we think through our own situations with their particular constraints and possibilities, and can we see, with conscious reflection, the choices we ourselves have made? This is the stance I suggest as we consider the big issue of how teachers negotiate standardized curriculum.

Let me first introduce Grace, whom we meet in Chapter 2, a teacher with nearly 30 years' experience who has taught kindergarten through second grade, and children with special needs, over her long career as a "primary specialist." This year she is teaching kindergarten. Grace is a quiet personality, warm and supportive of everyone: she doesn't like to criticize. She tells us she wants so much to introduce children to school in ways that make them *want* to come to school. She is known by her colleagues as an exemplary teacher, with a curriculum both emergent and rooted in the co-construction of a vibrant classroom community. How do you think Grace will approach the standardized curriculum, and how might it alter her pedagogy?

Chapter 3 portrays Corrine, another kindergarten teacher, but much younger and with only 5 years experience, and without the benefit of early childhood education as part of her teaching preparation. She is torn between the tension of whether to support young children's play and the generation of their own ideas and plans, or whether to teach children in traditional teacher-directed fashion. Corrine seesaws back and forth trying to balance conflicting notions of good practice for young children. Yet she finds the traditional teacher-directed curriculum boring, for her and for the children. She has found that she gets excited by pedagogical documentation. Last year she documented children's play, such as the children's spontaneous construction of a library in the block area, complete with handmade books and lists of names of children "having overdue books." From such documentation, her interest and belief in the significance of the play of young children deepened. What will she do with a standardized curriculum and its pressures?

In Chapter 4 we meet Janet, a first-grade teacher with a graduate degree in special education and 12 years of teaching experience in early childhood. She believes in a teaching practice that permits children to plan, to co-own the classroom with her, to initiate and create and learn technical, traditional aspects of schooling (such as use of capitals and periods in writing) informally in the course of meaningful activity. Janet talks excitedly about how perturbed she is about the rapid changes in education and the new expectations suddenly imposed on young children, some of which she feels are inappropriate. We get the sense she feels something immoral in the demands the curriculum makes on children. Vivacious and mature, she sounds distressed and worried. What will she do with her anguish, her sense of ethical dilemma, in the face of the imposition of a curriculum with which she disagrees?

As we meet Ann through Chapter 5, we first hear her voice—rich, clear, beautifully modulated. Another first-grade teacher, she has 15 years experience and a strong love of language arts and books. This year she is taking a course in ESL, and many of the children in the first stages of learning English are grouped in her classroom. She tells us she loves to read to the children four or five times daily, that she "would love to read to them all day long." She worries about time pressures due to the massiveness of the curriculum, but thinks of herself as offering an early childhood curriculum. What will her approach be like?

And here is Susan in Chapter 6, a young teacher of first grade in her ninth year of teaching during this research. She spent four years as a "long-term occasional" teacher (for maternity or illness leaves of several months) before she had her own classroom, and does not have an ECE background. She tells us her classroom includes many early childhood activities, such as a sandbox, an easel, and an art and science area, but that she has been unable to use them except during the last half-hour of the day, when she rotates groups through them while she does reading conferences. She has so much to do and so much to get through that she finds her time very tightly controlled to produce the necessary outcomes by the end of the year. We can tell she is tied to a tight production schedule, as indeed are many teachers. What is that like for her and the children, and what consequences can we see?

We meet Ellen and Penny in Chapter 7, team-teaching second grade in a double classroom. Ellen is a mature woman who moved to teaching in midcareer after decades of experience as a social worker. She has a two-year credential in ECE in addition to her teaching certificate and enters her third year of teaching during this study. Penny has been teaching for 12 years, her degree including a two-year specialty in children with special needs. They tell us how they struggle daily with the conflict of wanting to offer their young children meaningful experiences that can be understood in the context of their lives, and the press of the standardized curriculum that pushes them continually to think they must "cover" more content. Their teacher talk is of persistent time pressures and a sense of stressful worry about the possibility of not meeting curriculum requirements in the time required.

Last is Beth, a teacher with a classroom combining second and third grade, whom we meet in Chapter 8. Beth has 12 years teaching experience. She tells us her passion in teaching is science, that she builds her program around her science interests, that it works for her. She tells us she is interested in developing children's "critical thinking skills, like questioning skills" and wishes "to encourage their love of learning." She is also intrigued by her school's new time organization, with a two-hour block of uninterrupted time in the morning, followed by a long recess. How will the standardized curriculum fit here?

In Chapter 9 I analyze the range of ways in which these teachers in the early years are taking up a standardized curriculum and how they think their teaching has changed as a consequence. We will see four approaches among the eight participants, and I will attempt to tease out some of what compels teachers to take up the standardized curriculum in linear, segmented ways and what permits teachers to liberate themselves toward more developmentally appropriate practice. Here I also set the individual portrayals of these teachers in the broader theoretical context of the debate between holistic practices and prescriptive practices in the education of young children. Holistic practices are ones in which all parts are interconnected, rhythms of growth are permitted, and relationality, reciprocity, and emergent processes are given priority (Edwards, Gandini, & Forman, 1998; Franklin, 1999). Prescriptive practices are ones in which the parts are fragmented into linear production, with the production preplanned on a time schedule and presumed to be predictable and controllable (Bowers & Flinders, 1990; Franklin, 1999). Should building relationships, collaboration and creativity, planning and sharing power be fundamental to the experience of a child's education? Or should building a production schedule that "produces" a person with tightly specified technical skills be fundamental? Teachers in early childhood live out this debate in their daily practice, because teachers are embedded in these contradictory frameworks that are essential features of mainstream culture. How they work out the conflicting demands of these two frameworks for practice is the story of this book, each teacher both a unique exemplar (in that we would not expect any other teacher to be exactly like her) and also an exemplar of the general situation in which all teachers are caught. This book is the story of how eight individuals lived with this dilemma at the point in time during which the research was undertaken. Through reflecting on the detailed particulars for a handful of teachers, we also see the broader dilemmas faced by anyone who chooses to teach young children in schools in this time of standardized curriculum and assessment.

NOTES

✱ 1. In Canada, teachers complete a one-year program in education following an undergraduate degree to earn a B.Ed. that qualifies them to teach. An ECE specialization is an undergraduate degree in Child Study or a 2-year community college program plus undergraduate degree.

2. The Education Quality and Accountability Office (EQAO) of the government of Ontario evaluates third-grade children each May. For one week, a scripted curriculum assigned by the office is taught by all third-grade teachers, the children are tested on it, and the tests are scored by external provincial assessors. Scores on reading, writing, and mathematics are reported to schools and in the media.

CHAPTER 2

Grace

Sustaining Community in a Developmentally Appropriate Kindergarten

I begin with a portrayal of Grace because she so clearly exemplifies developmentally appropriate practice, and displays a strong match between her philosophy and teaching practices. She is recognized within her board for outstanding work in early childhood, confident yet striving always to reach for more. Grace has close to 30 years' experience teaching junior kindergarten (preschool) through fourth grade, including some years with children who are gifted and others with children with special needs. She has a B.A.

in History and Political Science, and additional qualifications as a Primary Specialist and in Reading and Special Education. In the year of our research together, Grace was teaching a morning kindergarten program for 5-year-olds and in the afternoons creating a new program, an Early Learning Center, for rotating groups of 4-year-olds each attending with a parent or caregiver. This program for 4-year-olds involved having parents, children, and possibly younger siblings join Grace in the classroom several times per week and, in addition, organizing a series of workshops for parents, and a series of screening assessments on children's vision, speech and language, dental hygiene, and hearing. The children in both programs were very diverse, coming from cultural backgrounds such as Punjabi, Korean, Gujarati, Twi, Arabic, Spanish, Cantonese, and Vietnamese. In addition, a first-grade child with special needs attended her morning kindergarten program. Here I will first offer a portrayal of her as a teacher constructing developmentally appropriate practice, and then show her stance toward the 1998 kindergarten document and how she works with it.

THE VIEW INTO GRACE'S CLASSROOM:
AN IMAGE OF DEVELOPMENTALLY
APPROPRIATE TEACHING

In the early childhood years in school, teachers with early childhood education background and philosophies attempt to construct a developmentally appropriate practice that is open and responsive to children (following their interests, skills, and capacities as individuals), recognizes and adapts to family and cultural background in addition to issues of child development, and wraps knowledge of these contexts into curriculum decisions in the classroom (Bredekamp & Rosegrant, 1992). To convey a sense of how this works in a school setting, I will show Grace in her classroom, and in discussions with me, by highlighting eight key aspects of her approach that together illustrate an exemplar of developmentally and culturally appropriate practice for very young children. These eight areas are:

1. Establishing a climate of psychological safety
2. Establishing a sense of community
3. Observing as a route to knowing the children, and to inform curriculum decisions
4. Supporting children's interests and knowledge
5. Supporting children's play and an emergent, responsive curriculum

6. Supporting children's problem solving, choices, and planning
7. Supporting parents
8. Reflecting on and developing her teaching practice

While this is not an exhaustive portrait of developmentally appropriate teaching (no mention is made of design of the space, or of specific developmental or cultural issues, for example), it is an attempt to highlight major facets of this practice.

Grace's classroom was a colorful, well-equipped space with an adjoining coatroom, bathrooms, and a door to the outside playground. L-shaped, the long and narrow main section was organized into several play areas (blocks, housekeeping, a carpet area for group work and play), and the shorter part of the L offered windows, and tables and chairs for table work such as drawing and writing, art activities, puzzles, and so forth. The walls of the long section had many cupboards, a sink with supplies for making tea nearby, and, mounted on the cupboard doors and walls, photographs or samples of the children's work carefully matted by Grace in bright colors. In the middle sat a bare-branched tree from which all manner of items, such as photos or drawings, might be suspended, in changing exhibits.

Establishing a Climate of Psychological Safety

Grace says that when children first encounter her and the classroom, her "first objective is for them to feel comfortable." To assist this sense of comfort, she has them visit with a parent before school begins. She ensures that in the first days of school they are doing "very nonthreatening types of things—the outdoor play, the sandbox, . . . the puzzles, the coloring, the toys that are out, most of them would be familiar or very easy to figure out." She describes how she introduces children to the washroom, asking the parent to go through it with the child on their initial visit; "but I also wanted them to know that I knew about those things, it was okay to ask me." As children begin school, Grace first wants to assure their comfort and meet basic needs, and wants children "to start to build some relationships with each other." She speaks of how she "wants them to *like* school," to be sure it's a place where "they want to come back to," a place where "they feel safe." When I visited in September, it amazed me that after only a week or so in school, 24 children were all playing happily, absorbed in interesting activities, and that there were no tears or difficulties at any point in the morning. I found this impressive, because it looked like a class that had functioned together for much longer.

Establishing a Sense of Community

An essential aspect of Grace's practice is the way she develops a sense of community among members of the class so that each child is both confident of her own visibility in the group while also encouraged to care for and support every other member. To convey this complex web of supportive social relationships, here is an observation from my field notes of Grace reading a story to a group of 4-year-olds attending the Early Learning Center. This is in April, when these 8 to 10 children have been attending twice a week for several weeks.

Eight children sit in a semi-circle around Grace as she reads a story about a balloon. Behind the children, on low chairs sit eight mothers or grandmothers, also enjoying the story and their children's delight in it. A ninth child listens from her mother's lap, not ready to join the group on the rug. Grace reads with great animation about a balloon getting bigger and bigger, and then WHOOooooosh (in descending tones).

"Now what happens to it?" The children don't quite understand the fact that her words and actions, alongside the picture, represent the air coming out of the balloon. She suggests they listen with their ears and repeats the passage. "So big, SO BIG, and WHOOooooosh. Did you hear it?"

"I heard it!" says the girl on Mom's lap.

The children participate with lively chatter, offering their ideas, interrupting the story frequently, and Grace lets them, gradually leading them back into the story. Sometimes she invites them to predict; for example, what will happen to the balloon when the child holds onto the string?

"I think it will go up!"

"I think he will let go."

"I think he will go to Mars."

"It's a Mars guy."

"It's an alien."

"I have lots of movies too!"

She helps them listen to each other. Someone says, "He has the powers."

"Who has the powers," says Grace, "the boy or the balloon?" The children all respond at once, so it is impossible to hear individual ideas, but Grace says of one child, "Oh she's thinking, she's thinking, isn't she!" Then some children spontaneously put up their hands to speak, and she compliments them. She continues, "Oh

Jessie, please wait. I'll ask you to speak in a minute. I won't forget you." She comes back to her shortly.

"Yes, Jessie, what did you want to say?"

"I love you."

"I love you, too," replies Grace.

After the story she plays a card game with numbers and gets the mothers to help the children understand how to pass the cards. It is not easy for the children to coordinate this action following the teacher's instructions. After two rounds of the game, Grace says, "That takes a lot of cooperation. I love the way you cooperated."

"Can we do it again?" says one girl.

"Oh yes, we'll do it another day, but I'm thinking the children need to go to activities." She selects a child to gather up the cards, and explains briefly to the parents what is happening, that the children are learning to take turns, to wait, "all these little things they are learning to do."

On the one hand she is teaching them the structure of group work in school. On the other, she is teaching them how to be visible in a large group both by cooperating with the process and by finding appropriate spaces/turns where individual contribution is welcomed. Grace shows the children with careful explicitness how she wants them to treat each other and her, and how each will be acknowledged within the framework of the collective. Continuously, she lets them know what pleases her and how well they are doing. Also, she does exactly what she says she will do, so they know that they can trust her. The necessary paradox here is that even as they adjust to being part of a large group, Grace assures each and every one that they are visible to her and to each other, that they belong.

Observing to Know Children and Inform Curriculum Decisions

Attentive observation of children has long been at the core of teaching practice in early childhood (Bredekamp, 1987; Bredekamp & Copple, 1997; Cohen, Stern, & Balaban, 1997; Edwards, Gandini, & Forman, 1998; Hendrick & Chandler, 1996; Hohmann, Banet, & Weikart, 1978; Montessori, 1964; Read & Patterson, 1980). Teachers of young children with early childhood backgrounds have generally experienced as part of their training some emphasis on observation and recording of children's development, interests, needs, and capacities. An aspect of the important notion of "appropriateness" is a teacher's ability to take into account developmentally and culturally appropriate expectations for young children, alongside the interests of children, and to use this knowledge in making curriculum decisions. Grace's attentive watching and listening to children is evident throughout the activity time when children are making self-initiated choices. Here is a snapshot of Grace in September, showing how observation is woven into her teaching process.

> Six children sit around a table drawing birthday pictures. Three children work on puzzles and one boy draws at a table nearby. Five boys make a shoulder-high structure with tinkertoy-like construction materials called "No-Ends." Four other boys play on the carpet laying out a complex train track. Three girls play, each alone, in housekeeping. Another sits by herself at the snack table eating a granny smith apple. A boy is describing his birthday picture to me. Grace moves around very quietly, crouched low. Sometimes she takes notes unobtrusively. Occasionally she gets her camera and takes a photograph. She moves with such quietness and talks so softly that it is hard to see where she is in the room. The children at the drawing table begin to sing scatological verses amid much laughter:
> "Happy Birthday to you,
> You smell so peouuw" . . .
> Grace is right there speaking softly to the perpetrator. But most of the time one cannot see her easily. Sometimes a child looks up and says, "Where's Mrs. Carter?"

An outsider to teaching might have no idea of the complex underlying structure already understood by the children that keeps the room functioning so that Grace can seemingly disappear into its activity: all eyes, ears, and continuous thinking, she takes notes and photos of interesting events; moves in on situations that require her assistance or structuring, helps children find things (a quiet child needs a chair to join the drawing table); and continuously observes and makes split-second decisions about where and when to act, what to let go, what to support. And each intrusion of hers is extremely efficient in that a very small amount of it works. The scatological remarks stop. When the boys at the train track complain, "He broke the track up," she goes slowly toward the very broken-up layout, asking, "Do you think someone can help fix it?" It begins to be fixed, and she leaves.

There is of course much more than observation at work here. This is a teaching practice with the highest levels of understanding of young children and artfulness in supporting their relationships and learning. But observation, built on a foundation of developmental knowledge and years of teaching experience, is a core process in sustaining the functioning of the room.

Supporting Children's Interests and Knowledge

Supporting children's interests and knowledge in the form of encouraging child-initiated activities has long been important to early childhood. This understanding combines the necessity for young children to be *active*, that is, able to use their entire body as they engage with the world, and to be able to act on the good ideas they generate, for these are the contexts of greatest motivation and learning for them (Hendrick & Chandler, 1996; Hohmann, Banet, & Weikart, 1978; Piaget, 1962). Two ways this emerges in Grace's classroom are (1) her emphasis on ensuring that every aspect of her curriculum is "relevant" to young children; and (2) her giving children permission to pursue child-initiated ideas within the overall framework of the collective process.

In ensuring the relevance or meaningfulness of classroom events to children's lives, she parallels important events in their lives, such as reading a picture book about birthdays on a Monday following a weekend when three children celebrated birthdays, and inviting them to draw something about their experience. On another occasion she saw an opportunity to introduce coins and money values when the children showed an interest in creating a store or restaurant out of the puppet theater. In these small examples one can see how important processes of schooling (such as reading, writing, and numeracy) are connected to events of interest to children that she has observed in their talk or play.

Giving permission to children to pursue a child-initiated idea in school is a more sophisticated development in a teacher's practice than merely offering choices of activity. Grace tells a story about such child-initiated activity at our first interview. On the way back from walking the attendance register down to the office, Kai heard a cheep and identified it as a cricket:

> You could just see him in the hall there—his head going—looking to see if he could see where it was. When we came back to the classroom and the children went off to activities, he went right to the door and probably was there about ten minutes before he came to me and said that he'd found the cricket. And I said, "Oh, we've got this container we can put it in, if you'd like to do that." So I helped him get it in the container. It was amazing all the things that he

could tell me about crickets. How they made their chirp by rubbing their wings together. How they hopped, and grasshoppers hopped too. And how he once caught a grasshopper and it squished and it had brown blood, so he thought crickets might have brown blood too because they hopped the same as grasshoppers. He shared this information at the end of the day with the other children just before they went home. The end of the week we let the cricket go free.

The children quickly realize that what they know about the world and what they are interested in are welcome contributions to Grace's classroom.

Supporting Children's Play and an Emergent Curriculum

One way of generating emergent curriculum is through recognizing children's interests in their play, observing to follow the children's lead, and *then* planning from what is observed (Jones, Evans, & Rencken, 2001). Such a curriculum is deeply meaningful to both children and adults because what is interesting is also what has powerful emotional content. But in addition, such curriculum also satisfies broader cultural expectations for what children "should" be learning in terms of literacy and numeracy, although the content may appear quirky or unconventional, linked as it is with specific interests of real children and teachers. It draws on children's most developed functioning in ways that are not prescribed or standardized, but organic and creative: everyone's good ideas have a place in such a curriculum (Carter & Curtis, 1999; Edwards, Gandini, & Forman, 1998; Jones & Nimmo, 1994). An example of supporting children's play and its emergence into curriculum arose in the block area, where an emphasis on boats developed. Grace told me how she and the student teacher worked with that interest.

The children were making a lot of boats, so I said to Jean, "We need to support that." I said, "I don't have boating things, we're not a boating family," but she has a pool in her backyard and she has those things. She brought in a float, she brought in oars back there, ropes, a lifejacket, and [we] watched how their play has changed. She brought books from the library. You just sit back there and write what they are saying, and you learn so much. With the two of us here, we can do that. You don't have that luxury when you're on your own in the classroom, so [I'm telling her,] "do this and enjoy this and see what a difference it makes." This morning what happened was they got into one of the books, *The Titanic*, and it unfolds, with eight pages that unfold and a four-page spread, and they were making the Titanic. They were using the book, Carol Anne, to check—the smokestacks, and all.

Grace comments that she supports the student teacher's efforts by taking photographs of the children's activity and notes of their conversations on days when Jean is away at her courses.

> One day a little guy had a clipboard and was writing things down and I said, "What are you doing?" And he said, "Well I'm the captain." And I said, "What job are you doing when you are writing?" And he said, "I have to write what's happening on the boat." And I said, "Oh you're keeping a log!" He knew that. They know so much.

Supporting Children's Activity Choices, Problem Solving, and Planning

Teachers with early childhood background understand that young children are developing important lifelong skills in being able to plan and organize themselves (important aspects of self-regulation) when they make decisions about what to do from a genuine array of choices, and when they generate solutions to everyday problems and anticipate consequences of their actions (Bredekamp & Copple, 1997; Hendrick & Chandler, 1996; Shure & Spivak, 1978). Grace comments on how these are all very important to her throughout the year, and explains how she is less involved with children's problem solving toward the end of the year because they are doing it on their own: "I've been there those beginning months to help them with that, to be a facilitator to say, 'Well, what could we do? Who's got some ideas about what we could do?' . . . Sometimes you still need to be there to help, but they're able to do much more of that on their own now." I ask her about making choices and planning, if they are still important to her at the end of the year or whether she is thinking in terms of more academic instruction at this point. "Oh, I expect them to choose more and plan more, to keep doing more of that. Not taking it away! And also to point out to them that that is what they are doing." She gives an example of how Min went one day and copied out all the children's names that started with M, like her own.

> Then she brought it to show me. So of course, we shared that with the group. That's the kind of thing you're looking for. Then she said, "Tomorrow I do D." I said, "Oh, so tomorrow you've got a

plan! You've got a plan already in your head that tomorrow you're going to write all the children's names that start with D!" The next day she did that. I didn't say anything, and she did that. So of course, in the group time before they left, I said, "Wow, do you remember yesterday Min said she was going to do this? She had a plan? And today (in a voice of great enthusiasm) she remembered her plan and she did it!"

Throughout each day there are multiple occasions when choice, problem solving, and planning are not only encouraged, but made explicit to the children as processes they are engaged in as they go about their activity. Grace thus teaches the children a metacognitive language to differentiate aspects of their thinking. It is interesting in this regard to note recent findings about growth patterns in the brains of young children, and the fact that in 3- to 6-year olds in one study, the "fastest growth rates occurred in frontal networks that regulate the planning of new actions" (Thompson, Gledd, Woods, MacDonald, Evans, & Toga, 2000, p. 190). The early childhood field has long made the inference that it is important to permit children many opportunities to plan events at this age, and these findings suggest that the inference is supported in the research base of neuroscience.

Supporting Parents

In early childhood, a relationship among teachers, children, and parents has always been considered fundamental to high-quality programs (Bredekamp & Copple, 1997; Edwards, Gandini, & Forman, 1998). The notion is that communication is reciprocal, that is, that parents have an impact on teachers as well as teachers having an impact on parents. Grace's commitment and extensive work to support parents is evident particularly through her work in creating the Early Learning Center on the one hand, and on the other, in her poignant comments on what she feels she has been unable to do in this particular year, which is to communicate as much with parents of the kindergarten class as she would normally expect to do.

It's the hardest year of my teaching because of the two programs. . . . For instance, in the kindergarten program, we would have had the parents in in the fall for a half-day visit. And then again in the spring, so they could see how the program and the children have changed as the year goes on. I wasn't able to do that. I haven't been able to do as many newsletters [to parents] as I would normally do.

She has not been able to fulfill her own sense of obligation to support parents this year in the kindergarten because her time outside class has been preoccupied by establishing the Early Learning Center program. With respect to this new program, she has acted as telephone receptionist, administrator who organizes multiple programs (described in the opening of the chapter), and the conductor of the programs. She commented, "I mean I almost gave up. I almost gave up."

She almost gave up because it was "just too hard" to get all of this organized in addition to running the morning kindergarten class. But Grace's commitment to supporting parents is such that she did not give up, and the programs for parents were considered highly successful by both participants and presenters. In addition, she commented in her feedback to the first draft of this account that her work with the families of the 4-year-olds led her to want to do more for the kindergarten families, once she "could see what a difference it made to have face-to-face contact, to have them there—not just phone calls and newsletters."

Her support for parents extends in many directions, not least in conversations with them about handling situations at home. She described a difficult child whose mother complained to her that the child said he was going to run away from home. What should she do? Grace tells me:

> And I said, "It's hard for me to say, but I'd almost say, 'Well, what are you going to take with you? Why do you need to run away?'" [I told her] "Don't get angry about it. Don't get upset about it." So what happened one day is he did pack his suitcase, and he went out, and she had told him that he couldn't go off his property. He went to the edge of their property and sat there with his suitcase. Just trying it out. And a couple of times she opened the door, and said, "B___, would you like to come back?" And eventually he did. He came back and had lunch and that was the end of it. But I have to believe I had a little bit of influence on how she dealt with all kinds of things to do with him.

Reflecting on and Developing Practice

Curriculum documents are but one source of new material that has influenced Grace in recent years. She tells me how influenced she has been by the Reggio Emilia Approach to educating young children, and how their principles have led her to think more carefully about how she uses her classroom environment, about links with the outdoor environment, about her intention to sustain and deepen relationships and to develop her documentation skills. "My view of the child as rich, powerful and strong has certainly been strengthened." Here are two examples to provide the flavor of the leading edge of Grace's teaching practice, and how she thinks about these events.

While Grace has for many years taken photographs of children in activity and displayed them, she has in recent years become more conscious of how such photographs and records of children's conversation act as vehicles by which children have access to their own thinking. In this incident, when the children were playing boats, she describes how a photograph was used by children to make a connection.

> They had this discussion one day of who was going to be the captain, because they sometimes use the steering wheel; and Lela, a little girl, was determined that she was going to be the captain, that she hadn't had a turn to be the captain. And Nigel said to her, "Lela, you have so. Look right here at this picture." And there's a picture on the back wall and she's the captain of the boat in the picture. And I thought, oh my gosh, I'd never seen them use the photographs to support their argument. But he'd obviously looked at it before because he knew it was there and could point to that resource. That was great.

She sees that the documentation makes their past experience visible to the children, offering a recursive loop that deepens the present.

Second, the notion of putting relationships at the core of programs, while not novel in early childhood thinking, has received new challenge from the early childhood community's engagement with the inspiration of Reggio Emilia: the early childhood community sees in Reggio Emilia a practice that has developed notions of relationality far deeper than the North American mainstream had imagined (see, for instance, Cadwell, 1997, 2003; Curtis & Carter, 2003; Fraser, 2000; Hendrick, 1997; Wien, 1997, 2000). The notion of teachers taking responsibility to deepen relationality refers to relationships in many directions—among children, children and natural environment, children and materials, children and multiple cultures. Grace's description of an event at the final day celebration for the Early Learning Center shows her sensitivity to this principle.

> We had several Punjabi grandfathers attend the final day and we were making ice cream sundaes. These men like to sit and chat with each other in their own language—it's hard to draw them in—and they didn't come get a sundae, so I went to them and said, "come on" and waved them over to help themselves. They looked at each other,

and came over. I have a student teacher visiting who also speaks Punjabi, and she was amazed, because after they had their sundaes they went and joined the children to wash up their dishes at the sink. She said they would never have done this in their own homes.

Grace was pleased they felt they could take part in what all the other parents and families were doing even though it might be strange. She commented, "I don't want to change their traditions, I just want them to feel part of the 'school culture' and participate at their own comfort level."

GRACE'S STANCE TOWARD THE STANDARDIZED CURRICULUM

"It's not going to drive my program"

How does a kindergarten teacher like Grace work with ministry documents and expectations for kindergarten? "I don't go from the documents to the kids: I go from the kids to the documents." Grace has of course seen many documents come and go throughout a nearly-30-year career in teaching. As we look at the document together, she notes that there is very little in it that is problematic or a particular surprise: the content is as she would expect for kindergarten. I remind Grace of my interest in discovering how teachers in early childhood years are working with the new documents and ask her whether it serves, for example, as a background document that she knows but does not dwell on, or whether she worries about her classroom representing in some way all the elements within the document. "I'll probably have to refer to this more this year because I'm new in kindergarten since this [document] was developed. . . . but it's not going to drive my program." In other words, the documents are not, for Grace, the starting point. Rather, her starting points are the children, their families and cultural backgrounds, and her own extensive professional knowledge and experience about teaching, children's development, appropriate curriculum, and her practical knowledge about how to construct a classroom community that functions superbly as it promotes learning. She notes that all the listed expectations are the usual things that "will happen, just by giving the kids the kind of experiences you would normally give them in Kindergarten. Look at this one: 'describe local habitats—ponds, nests, and trees.' Well, when we go to the woodlot we'll be talking about these kinds of things." She acknowledges that much is involved in how the documents are interpreted, that, for instance, when it says "investigate familiar geographical features" she understands that to mean rolling down the hill in your schoolyard in summer or sledding on it in winter. If we think of the possibilities that teachers see for themselves, we could say that Grace sees her teaching reflected in the documents. She can see the relation between its abstract summary (geographical features) and the real-life experiences (rolling down a hill) that she supports. She notes in addition that if there was anything problematic, "I'd probably—depending on what it was—I'd think about whether it was developmentally appropriate for the kids."

"If it doesn't have relevance, they're not going to remember it anyway"

I find it interesting that Grace takes into account the role of *forgetting* in learning. The human organism is designed to discard information that it does not need to attend to (see Norretranders, 1998, for a summary of research on recent understandings about consciousness) and learns, in part, by making its own connections between what it already understands and new information (Caine & Caine, 1997; McCain & Mustard, 1999). Grace recognizes that material to which the child cannot make a reasonable connection will not be meaningful and thus will not be learned. As an example, she asks, "In Grade One, for them to know that John A. MacDonald was the first Prime Minister of Canada, how relevant is that to a 6-year old?" In the language of early childhood, this fact is not developmentally appropriate, because children's understanding of historical time, of nations, and of structures of government is limited. And what is learned by rote is the best candidate for forgetting, because it cannot become attached to deep structures of meaning in the mind.

Nowhere do ministry documents (that I am aware of) take into account the role of forgetting in humans; but sensibly, how could they? They could hardly say the curriculum will be learned, then forgotten, although adults know the truth of this. The documents treat learning as cumulative, as in part it is. This view of the mind as accumulating knowledge takes as its metaphor the mechanical machine to be filled. While Grace takes the documents very seriously, she has the confidence and knowledge to override on occasion a low-priority expectation that in her judgment is misplaced. Yet the larger question remains: what do we do with the fact the curriculum documents acknowledge one facet of learning but not others?

A Caring Community Where Power Is Shared

When I asked Grace whether she thinks the documents capture the whole of what she is attempting to do for the children and their families, she responded, "No, no, I don't think so. There's a lot that no curriculum document can ever capture." What else is missing in these curriculum documents? One aspect is the construction of a group life that is caring, responsible, and civil. Grace notes:

> I would hope I do a lot more than what is in there [the documents], especially in the realm of social and emotional [development], particularly in that. This group of [kindergarten] children, they are amazing, the way that they care about each other. The way that they support and help each other is just phenomenal. You would think that they've been working together for a couple of years, truly, truly.

This accomplishment in the children arises out of the climate of psychological safety and caring for the community established from the outset with such care, commitment, and explicitness by this teacher. These are part of her pedagogy, and she believes they really matter.

The curriculum documents give the impression that the most important aspect of school is the learning of individual children. From the teacher's perspective, however, individual learning of expectations established by the government is not the fundamental issue. The fundamental issue is establishing the underlying structure that will convince a large number of disparate individuals to function together to carry out purposes decided by the teacher. This orchestration of the group around shared purposes that will result in learning requires specific capacities in the teacher—projection of energy and intent (comparable to an actor); understanding of strategies of movement and use of space (like a football or basketball player); continuous thinking on one's feet (planning, organizing, problem solving); and the capacity to inspire wildly different individual children to take up the teacher's agenda. If the teacher cannot get the children to function together as a group, little productive learning can occur. It is an odd dislocation that these documents address individuals only, but that teachers' work is first and foremost with large groups.

An aspect of the classroom that documents do not address is the fundamental underlying structure of power relations that determines how the group will live together for the year. In Grace's room, locations of power are shared. Children know there are places where their good ideas, whether catching a cricket or copying out names, will be welcomed. Each individual learns to have a commitment to the whole, while held in the safety net of knowing Grace will take overall responsibility: a child wants to play a group game again, and while assuring the girl her wish will be met at some point,

Grace recognizes the larger group has been sitting long enough. The needs of the larger group are met, while also acknowledging the interests of the individual within it. Such a pedagogy ensures individual learning within collective life.

An Enduring Patience

Grace demonstrates confidence that the expectations that the documents describe are indeed experiences that will occur naturally within her program. By *naturally* I mean that in the course of children's play and self-selected activities many occasions will arise where she can extend the expectations in the document by offering materials and information that connect directly to their play, and the experiences for language learning, numeracy, science and so forth that are contained therein. In this regard, I hypothesize that her sense of time is more expansive than some teachers: "We have a long 10 months," Grace said at one point. She knows from the long body of her teaching that all the expectations the document encapsulates are part—but not all—of that rich 10-month experience in her classroom. She has, thus, a capacity to wait, coupled with attentive observation of children, and to think or reflect before planning. She plans from life in her classroom, in addition to incorporating information on the major symbol systems of society (reading, writing, numeracy, etc.) that the child must gradually master. Her practice thus remains open ended, developmentally appropriate, responsive. It preserves reciprocity in power relations, that is, a mutual give and take that shares power to enact with children, while simultaneously taking responsibility for shaping the framework for the whole.

Parents as Partners

The ministry requirement for kindergarten at this time was that there be some form of reporting to parents: in Grace's school this was an anecdotal report at the end of the year. In addition, Grace invites parents to two parent–teacher conferences, one in the fall, one in the winter. She conducts these as mutual conversations about the child in which parents are consulted about what will be written down as a record of their conference:

> You start off with a blank sheet and tell the parents, "I'm going to take some notes as we are chatting; if there's something I'm not writing down as we chat that you would like me to include, please tell me." On issues where I've brought it up, I'll say to the parent

after we've talked about it, "Is it all right if I write this?" Or "How about if I write it this way? Would you agree with that?" Sometimes I even say "How would you like me to say that?"

Again, power is shared in a mutual way and there is a commitment to a "we." She describes how she and the parents together choose one goal for the child for the term, and how this goal might or might not be academic. It would be whatever was most pressing for both, such as learning to tie shoes, or taking responsibility for bringing library books home and back to school, or building friendships with other children, with the possibility that there might be a more academic goal for the second term, but not necessarily. Whatever the goal, it would be reviewed in later conferences or reports. Grace commented that she is aware of other kindergarten teachers who believe they must use checklists or make up a formal report card with grades on academic areas, but this has not been her experience.

CONSTRAINTS, CHOICES, AND POSSIBILITIES

If we reflect on the constraints and possibilities that Grace sees in her teaching, we can see that she does not view the ministry curriculum documents as a problem, a sort of "dictator," but rather as a guide describing aspects—but not the totality—of her program. The constraints that she mentions (not being able to build sufficient contact with her kindergarten parents) arise out of the fact that she was creating two separate programs, one of them new. She sees many creative possibilities in her teaching, from her fundamental emphasis on the construction of a caring community, a "civil society" in her classroom, to creating the Early Learning Center as she saw fit, and designing the registration for next year's kindergarten as a rich, dynamic event rather than a bureaucratic process. She designed it with gifts and activities for the children to do to welcome them, added screening personnel to check the children, and included refreshments for the adults. When I asked Grace what permitted her to continue to teach in full and creative ways, designing programs and communities, she mentioned the impact of others on her. She had learned how to teach this way from ECE resource consultants years ago. Those resource consultants are long gone from the school board, due to cutbacks. Also important is the impact of strong ECE colleagues in the field. But the key element is the support of her principal. Grace described her principal as someone who will listen, who visits her classroom and knows what's going on, and "who will support me in action"—whether talking to a parent about the necessity of monitoring a 15-month old baby in the Learning Center, or supporting her beautifully designed and welcoming registration for kindergarten.

There can be no doubt that Grace is an exemplar of an outstanding teacher for the early childhood years. Her continuing presence in an education system under enormous duress should give hope to beginning teachers that it is possible to construct and sustain a teaching practice that combines regulated expectations with developmental knowledge, ongoing reflection, care for children and families, and a commitment to community within diversity.

CHAPTER 3

Corrine

Teacher Direction or Developmental Appropriateness in Kindergarten

Corrine is a young teacher who was in her fourth year of teaching kindergarten during our research together. She had started with a traditional academic approach using worksheets, because this was what she saw in her school, and shifted gradually toward more developmentally appropriate practice under the influence of an exemplary colleague. Her principal had some early childhood background and was supportive. The year of our research was her second year of using the new ministry expectations for curriculum. Previous to her kindergarten teaching, Corrine had spent two years as a supply teacher. Her Bachelor of Education degree is at the Junior/Intermediate level (Grades 4–10), and her undergraduate degree, in Mathematics and Psychology. She noted, "None of my teaching [preparation] is in early childhood." In addition, she was the only kindergarten teacher in the school. This chapter highlights, thus, a relatively inexperienced teacher, without early childhood background, who had altered her teaching from academic to more developmentally appropriate ways and now attempts to incorporate new curriculum expectations. In this fourth year of teaching, how has her teaching practice evolved, how does she approach the new curriculum expectations, and what tensions, worries, successes, and concerns arise for her?

THE VIEW INTO CORRINE'S CLASSROOM

Corrine's kindergarten space was a double-sized rectangular classroom entered through huge double glass doors. It was so big, with so much in it, that it was hard to take it in. It felt like a space for 2 teachers and 50 children, whereas she was alone in it with about 20 children. Across from the glass doors was an exit to a playground of empty asphalt, an empty field beyond. Inside the door, a set of tricycles and other outdoor equipment was stored adjacent to the sandbox. The middle of the long room held tables and an arrangement of shelves with manipulatives, plasticene, art supplies, and so forth. One end of the room held the teacher's desk, a piano, and an open rug area for whole-group work. Across from this carpet was the house center and an open tiled area for block play, with coat cubbies along the side wall used as part of the block storage. At the other end of the long room, far away, was a puppet theater and water play, with snack tables beside the area of hooks and cubbies actually used for coats.

Both morning and afternoon classes appeared relatively homogenous, without high diversity during this particular year, but in fact 12 out of 40 children had ESL backgrounds. With one or two exceptions, all children were from families associated with mainstream culture (white, middle-class). I would describe Corrine as a lively, articulate teacher with spunk. It was courageous of her to invite me to attend her more difficult class, one including a number of "wild" little boys whom she was having difficulty settling into productive activity.

> On an afternoon in November, after returning from the library, Corrine sits with four children on the rug pursuing a retelling of "The Three Bears." Four children play at the sandbox, several girls work at the cut and paste table, and several more in the dramatic play area, and two boys are running trucks up and down the entire length of the long side of the room, making huge noises, as if it was their job to fill up the entire space with as much sound and motion as possible. We have agreed that I shall focus my observations on the "wild boys." Soon two other boys join in, and the four are spinning cars and trucks at each other, the cars crashing, parts falling off and spilling about. Corrine is far away.
>
> "You're not allowed to do that," a girl sitting nearby says to them.
>
> Large cars fly up and down the side of the room, crashing, banging into each other. It is extremely noisy, like outdoor play. Corrine is preoccupied with a small group "miles" away, and the children do not know me. I get out some large hollow blocks and make a ramp, which the boys immediately begin to use, one boy adding blocks to make it higher. I start to make an end wall to stop the cars now flying off the ramp, and a boy quickly gets the idea and continues building the wall. As I take these actions, I am thinking about Kamii and DeVries' work (1993) showing how experiences with ramps, effort, and distance provide understandings of informal physics.
>
> "We're playing jumping cars!"
>
> "Look out!"
>
> "No! You can't do it that way!"
>
> "Guys, I'm always first, I'm always first."
>
> Six of the "wild boys" settle into a simple pattern of shooting their car off the ramp to see how far it will go. Wild activity still, but it has direction and a focus. Liam begins using a hand signal to stop others from shooting their cars when he goes to repair the backstop, and the five boys wait in line. A good sign, I think, nice self-regulation.
>
> "I'm number ten!"
>
> "I'm number sixty-one."

"I'm number sixty!"

"I'm ten." This is the second time he says it.

"But I'm first."

"Oh, you're number sixteen."

"No, I'm number twenty-eight."

"I think, Liam, I'm number ten."

Several boys (4, 10) keep their numbers firmly, as if grasping that it identifies their car, like a race car number, while other boys' numbers slide around in exploration, and with the inference a higher number is better. Some seem to mix ordinal and cardinal functions. While the activity feels wild, I can see lots of order in it, and lots of curriculum possibilities as I observe, but I am very glad when Corrine appears on the scene.

While this view of the classroom shows the "wild boys," who treat the classroom like a giant playground containing only them, three-quarters of the group was functioning in ways comfortable to teachers in school settings. When Corrine appeared, the boys responded quickly and enthusiastically to her request, which we will pick up later. The difficulty with the highly active children is that they make everyone else in the room invisible, and I had enormous appreciation for Corrine's stamina in staying with the group with which she was working, and in attending to the other three-quarters of the room while the activity of the "wild boys" took over the soundscape of the room. In her feedback on our first draft, Corrine commented that this group of children could "easily demand most of my time and distract other children" and that this fact continued most of the year.

Changes in Corrine's Teaching Approach

Since Corrine had no background in her teacher preparation program for working with young children, she began her teaching of kindergarten by looking around her to see what other such teachers were doing. She happened to see a traditional academic style using plenty of worksheets, and that is how she began.

Developmental knowledge, I guess I'm getting it as I go along. I've never had any formal training in this. There aren't any resource teachers [now] who seem to know about kindergarten and developmentally appropriate practice.[1] And because I'm working on my own, I have no one to bounce ideas off of, so sometimes I learn things about children because I've been working with them for a few years.

I started off very traditional, everybody did worksheets. I rarely had time to observe children's play because I was too busy administering worksheets. That was before the [new] curriculum, because that's how I saw everyone else doing it.

In addition to worksheets she adopted the traditional cultural units, such as "All About Me" and "Bears." She quickly found this approach unsatisfactory, and met an interesting colleague, known for exemplary work, who taught very differently. On two different occasions she told me:

I was kind of bored with worksheets. I wanted to do things more developmentally appropriately.

I was getting bored and I thought if I was getting bored, the children must be too.

Also, she realized that for some children the worksheets were redundant: "Some kids knew the alphabet, and why should I sit them down and make them do a worksheet?" When she read the first draft of this account, Corrine added, "I also started realizing through reading about DAP, that worksheets are the least effective way for children who don't know the alphabet to learn it. I started to look for different teaching strategies."

Boredom, taking into account the knowledge that children brought with them to school, and a colleague who could provide links to teachers with more early childhood experience opened up other possibilities to her. "And my goal last year was to run the whole program without doing a worksheet. I haven't done one yet this year either [by November]." Her colleague encouraged her to get off the abstract paperwork, and also invited Corrine to join a professional group of teachers who could support her interests in a richer, more responsive teaching practice.

Conflict Between Play and Teacher Direction

In attempting a more developmentally appropriate, responsive teaching approach, Corrine was drawn into the necessary tension of puzzling out whether to impose teacher-directed activities (in her case, using checklists as assessment), or whether to support contexts that encouraged children's play and self-initiated activity, using observational techniques for assessment. As I have noted elsewhere (Wien, 1995), this tension between play and teacher-directed activity is one that early childhood teachers live with continuously—the weight of society seeming to insist on academic instruction (Elkind, 1990) and the press of the early childhood field arguing that an academic approach is inadequate for young children. It is inappropriate for children because it does not reflect the research base on how children learn (Bredekamp & Copple, 1997; Burts, Hart, Charlesworth, & Kirk, 1990; Duckworth, 1996; Hendrick & Chandler, 1996; Piaget, 1971; Santrock, 1996; Vygotsky, 1978), is not congruent with recent understandings about brain development in neuroscience (Caine, 1997; Thompson et al., 2000), and is extraordinarily limited as a pedagogy for working with young children (Dyson, 1993; Edwards, Gandini, & Forman, 1998; Gallas, 1994a; Hendrick & Chandler, 1996; Jones & Nimmo, 1994; Smilansky, 1990). In Corrine's case, ignorance fueled by boredom and recognition of prior learning in children led her to seek a more sophisticated practice. Such individual cases in early childhood education reflect the broader conflict within mainstream education between contradictory frameworks for teaching practice: on the one hand, the positivist, rational view of the learner as a consumer and education as incremental, quantitative, and cumulative; and on the other hand, the view of the learner as a complex living organism interconnected with other complex systems, an active agent responding in a dynamic, organic, holistic world (Davis & Sumara, 1997; Filippini, 1997; Heshusius & Ballard, 1996).

For Corrine, this struggle occurred in her uncertainty about whether to allow children to play in self-initiated activities or whether to impose teacher activities that they were required to do.

> I do have activities that I impose on the children, but I also give them time for play. So I'm trying to balance the two approaches. I also have to send home a program letter each term outlining the expectations that will be addressed and how they will be assessed.

She continues that one of the reasons she uses teacher-directed activities that all children must do is the requirement that she report on how *all* the children have met the selected expectations. She does not find that children meet the *same* expectations through play. She also says she's somewhat unsure how to respond when children play—when to step in, when to extend, when to ask a question, when to stay out altogether.

Corrine also commented that she had wanted to do projects with the children but didn't get to that because of additional school responsibilities: she was Chair of the Primary Division (K–3) and involved in administrative decisions around staffing and budgets. And the provision by the board of a series of checklists on the new expectations had the initial impact of making Corrine think she must assess each expectation via the checklists, and how could she do that without giving tasks to assess? Simultaneously, she provided an ample play time in which children chose activities from a rich array of material. She noted that her observation skills were sharper, and she had developed the habit of frequently taking photographs of children's play activities and writing running records of their conversation. The year of our research, she felt she had developed this skill of close attention and documentation of children much further, and was highly attuned to the children's play, its benefits for development, and what it demonstrated to her about the children: "I'm getting better at the daily stuff—this day this happened, and this day this happened—and seeing why it's important." She noticed, for instance, that some of the girls who are "behind" in language areas such as recognizing letters of the alphabet or book knowledge are nevertheless "really good ideas people" who "organize the kids" in play and show "a lot of leadership skills." She felt she had a better understanding of them through play: "I could see their strengths easier, whereas many teacher-directed activities have a narrow focus and sometimes show only their weaknesses." She noted that the children who cannot play well and "disrupt the other kids" are not as mature, not as comfortable in their adjustment to school as many children; "I'm worried because they can't play that well." She had made an interesting connection between children's play and children who function well at school tasks:

> I have some photos of children playing doctor, firefighter, mechanic. You see, those are my high-level ones [children] who are really applying it [understandings about community helpers], and that's my documentation for that unit, those children who are going beyond the whole-group discussion of the topic or the story.
> They're really applying it [their knowledge]. So, I thought, it's that dramatic play, that play that really tells you who will be your A's in Grade One.

This is the same argument made by Smilansky (1990), who presents research findings of close connections among high imagination and representation of ideas in kindergarten, and school achievement in mathematics and reading in second grade. Smilansky reminds us that much of school (history, mathematics, literature) requires an ability to imagine—other places, peoples, ideas, times not present—and it is this highly developed skill of representation that children develop in play.

Corrine also notices that the children can function at higher levels in self-initiated activity than they can when the teacher imposes the same activity:

> [Minta] . . . doesn't like doing anything that's teacher-selected. I was focusing on sorting one week and all the children were expected to complete a sorting activity with me. When it was her turn to work

with me, she was reluctant and wanted to leave. Later that week, she decided to go with a group of friends and start sorting. This was significant for two reasons: she was working with the other kids— she'd been working on her own [previously]—and because she was doing an activity I wanted her to do, but on her own initiative.

This fact, too, is noted by many developmental theorists (Donaldson, 1992; Vygotsky, 1978), that tasks that adults impose on young children can block children's access to their own knowledge of the world, but that this understanding visibly emerges when children choose the activity themselves in the company of peers. Vygotsky's famous phrase about play, that children walk a head taller than themselves (1978) when they play, captures the sense that the leading edge of children's intellectual functioning is present in self-initiated activity. They can do more in play than outside it. This difference in capacity, depending on context, is one of the reasons why those knowledgeable about early childhood insist that play and child-initiated activity be part of children's learning settings. To remove child-initiated activity with peers (as well as adults) reduces the child's opportunities to function at his or her leading edge of thought. The work of the educators of Reggio Emilia, and those inspired by them, illuminates the astounding results when child-initiated activity with peers is fully supported by teachers in reciprocal ways (Cadwell, 1997, 2003; Davoli & Ferri, 2000; Edwards, Gandini, & Forman, 1998; Hendrick, 1997; Malaguzzi, 1996; Vecchi, 2002; Wien, 1998).

Feeling pulled in conflicting directions in her teaching, yet attempting to make her teaching increasingly developmentally appropriate in a school context that has recently become standardized, how, then, does Corrine approach assessment in kindergarten?

Corrine's Assessment Practices

Corrine had developed one of the most comprehensive, carefully kept, and complex sets of assessment practices I have encountered in the school system. She had a huge binder with several kinds of data consistently collected. First, she had developed checklists of expectations for the subject areas described in the kindergarten curriculum document—mathematics, language, science and technology, the arts, and social studies (Ministry of Education and Training, 1998). Some sheets included specific criteria on one side and space for observations about children on the other, on such items as "curiosity and willingness to explore and experiment," "awareness of natural surroundings," "awareness of patterns in daily life," and so forth. Second, Corrine had a process for gathering up daily anecdotal observations during play on a sheet that she called "At a Glance," a paper with a small square for each child in which she could jot quick notes on daily activity. Weekly she cut up these squares and pasted them in a cumulative folder for each child. In addition to these checklists/observations sheets on expectations and the anecdotal "At a Glance" observations, she was also constructing classroom narratives using documentation techniques from teacher research—photographs, transcripts of tape-recorded conversations, and notes on conversations among children. From the latter materials she would choose photographs and accompanying text to put on the walls to share with the children, reflecting the children's work back to them. Such reflection permits children to think again about their work (Edwards, Gandini, & Forman, 1998; Hendrick, 1997). She would also select some of these situations to retain in a binder in a more fully developed narrative of classroom events, accompanying the observed data with her own comments about its importance and making connections between events and curriculum expectations.

One such narrative involved the children making a surprise party for another child, who had had her birthday several weeks previously:

> So on their own initiative, they went to the cut and paste center, made decorations, made a present, went to the playdough [center], made a playdough cake, and then they presented Marilyn with this. They sang Happy Birthday, they did it all. They were able to organize themselves and present that to Marilyn.

Corrine shows me the narrative in photos and text, the playdough cake with Popsicle stick candles, bits of playdough shaped into flames on the ends. She continues:

> Then I wrote my reflection on it. "This scenario demonstrates the children's ability to plan and organize themselves in dramatic play. They were able to use their shared experience of a birthday party to implement the sequence of events necessary to have a party—preparation, then the events. . . ."
> And then I also noted some Kindergarten expectations that would be met:
> "Sharing responsibility for planning classroom events";
> "Using pictures and sculptures to represent ideas";
> "Making preparations for performances."

Corrine is taking great care here to demonstrate to the outsider the connections between classroom events and the abstract expectations in the ministry document. The intention is that the outsider will understand what these expectations mean in her program. This detailed work to make her program visible to those outside the experience illuminates explicitly and graphically how these expectations are met.

A second narrative in photographs and text picks up on the "wild boys" and their "jumping cars" activity. When Corrine joined the boys' activity, she asked them to tell her what they had done, getting out the tape recorder to record their talk. She said the presence of the recorder always helped them talk one at a time. After they told her about "the jump" and wanting the cars "to go off the ramp, *over* the wall," one boy said, "I know, we'll make a bridge!" Corrine said she asked him:

> "How will you do that?"
> "Put the blocks under, and put them on top, and then you'll get squares." So [continues Corrine] he had a plan in mind of what he was going to do, so that gave them another focus for the next part of their play session. And then they built the bridge, which was tall rectangular blocks, all lined up with rectangular blocks laid across the top. And it was quite long, it was an L-shape, and it went all the way over to the wall.
> Looking at the photographs, I commented:
> "It really is a bridge. It's like a trestle bridge, isn't it? It's as high as their waist and the long blocks [on top] make a kind of highway where their cars can go way up in the air."

This kind of documentation is not only useful for place-holding memories about the evolution of children's activity, it is helpful to show parents during parent conferences, and outsiders who might wonder what useful things could be done in kindergarten play. It also sparks further complex play in the children: Corrine put the photograph of the bridge on the wall, and found that it inspired "more bridge building and road making," pushing forward the level of block play. She found, too, that the morning class was motivated by the photograph of the afternoon class, saying, "[We] want to build that like the afternoon class." This serious documentation of observable phenomena in her classroom allowed us to discuss her children, the program, and the connections between activity and curriculum in much more depth and elaboration than possible without this data. Corrine also found that constructing these narratives in photographs and text to document classroom life had been a pleasure, in the midst of her sense of overwhelming responsibilities that drew her attention away from the classroom: "I didn't mind spending an evening writing up stories and putting the photographs together. Actually I was happy when I finished this. . . . I have something that shows how my practice has changed and what I've learned about kindergarten." While pleased with her commitment to preserve and study the children's self-initiated activity, she regretted that she had not been able to move beyond this documentation to develop the projects she had hoped could happen in a more developmentally appropriate classroom.

CORRINE'S STANCE TOWARD THE STANDARDIZED CURRICULUM

Corrine thinks that the new kindergarten curriculum (Ministry of Education and Training, 1998) in part allowed her to refrain from doing some of the traditional units (like "All About Me") and focus on bigger topics: it opened up new curriculum possibilities for her.

> In some ways it's [the curriculum] gotten better because I've had to focus and make it more meaningful in order to connect everything together. I have to address all areas of the curriculum—we have to talk about science [now], we have to talk about the arts.

She had, for instance, chosen a focus on trees in the fall, and the class had been observing changes, attending to details of trees, and sketching trees and plants. She had learned from this that Minta, for example, understood that plants and trees have a food system carrying materials from roots through stems to leaves, and Corrine was astonished at what she learned about children's knowledge from the sketching and talk about trees. Thus the addition of expectations in science and the arts in kindergarten directed her attention to those areas and offered new curriculum possibilities to her. The focus on trees, for example, led to a painted mural on trees and animal homes that integrated art and science in the fall, and in the spring, a parent donated a tree that they planted on Earth Day.

She noted that the new curriculum "kind of threw me at first, especially the assessment and all these checklists." The checklists were materials provided by her board. However, in her second year with the checklists, she felt that they were not meant to be taken so literally, but were intended as guides, not absolutes, and she felt freer to develop her assessment more creatively. At the same time, she believed her assessment practices were "much richer" than previously, both because she was observing play more carefully and because "now I'm realizing what's more important—those connections kids are making."

> I always had a camera, but this year I'm using it more systematically. This year, I'm also playing with the tape recorder. So I'm pulling in more. I'm kind of getting better in spite of the curriculum.

The phrase "in spite of the curriculum" clearly reflects the tension she feels about being pulled in conflicting directions by contrasting frameworks for practice: as she tries to work in more developmentally appropriate ways, the checklists and linear expectations pull her toward a rationalist, mechanistic way of working with young children. The continuing development of more developmentally appropriate assessment practices, using observation techniques to document and study children's activity, and simultaneously the focus on board checklists for expectations, shows how both threads of the conflicting frameworks for practice are interwoven in the daily work of this teacher.

Although the new curriculum opened up new topics for her, she had concerns about it. One concern was what she thought was omitted from the document but that nonetheless requires a considerable focus of attention from the teacher: "I don't think there's enough emphasis on developing friendships, relationships, and the kind[s] of play children engage in. That's not in there anymore. . . . It's really not in there anymore, but it's so important." While she believed that some important areas of children's lives had been omitted or underemphasized, she also felt that some of what was included as curriculum expectations was "just stupid." Corrine's notion of "just stupid" expectations both shows her developing stance toward the ministry documents and unintended limitations in the document. My present hypothesis is that the combination of (1) expectations laid out subject by subject in fragmented lists and (2) a new emphasis on piecemeal assessment shapes teachers' responses to the documents. How does it shape their response? To be comprehensive, teachers are initially pulled into believing they must address and evaluate every single expectation singly in some way. Yet the expectations are drawn from many different levels of human functioning, as this example shows.

> I'm not going to try to cover every expectation anymore. Some of them, I'm not even going to sit down and assess anymore. It's just stupid.
>
> *Which ones are stupid?*
>
> Not stupid, but things that I can talk about but not [have to] sit down and figure out if they know it.
>
> *Are they too general?*
>
> Well, everybody figures out what the weather is like! Everybody knows by the end of fall, you need a winter coat! You don't need the

weather there [on the curriculum] to figure that out! . . . To sit down and assess them on it because it's a curriculum bullet is stupid.

Such expectations, thus, are too trivial. It is as if the curriculum developers were asked to include everything a child could be expected to know by the end of kindergarten, but nowhere is there recognition that the child arrives at school with considerable knowledge of the world and this knowledge does not have to be retaught. Part of the teacher's job is figuring out what to teach and what not to teach, because it has already been learned. Neither does the document differentiate types of understanding, such as tacit knowledge (absorbed by the body, e.g., put on more clothing when cold) or social knowledge (e.g., people wear coats and boots in winter); nor distinguish physical knowledge (understanding the physical properties of objects) from intellectual knowledge (the major symbol systems such as written language and mathematics). Thus the expectation that children know something is different from the expectation that it be taught and assessed, and Corrine can see that difference and respond to it sensibly.

Recognizing the Standardized Curriculum in Classroom Events

What Corrine understands at this point in time in terms of working with the ministry expectations is the necessity of constantly building up connections between her observations of children and the abstract expectations, showing what those expectations look like in classroom life. She finds that the abstract expectations, such as "planning and organizing," may be linked with a specific subject area, like science in the document, whereas she will observe it in the classroom in some other area:

> If they're playing a lot with art materials, that's where the higher level thinking is going to come out. And another child is playing with blocks all the time—they're going to "experiment with techniques and materials"—which is in the arts curriculum—but [they're doing it] with the blocks.

She has, thus, a sense of looking for bigger, more important expectations across the curriculum, rather than isolating them in specific curriculum areas, as the document seems to suggest. Here is an example of how she views herself as a teacher having to synthesize classroom events and curriculum expectations:

> Well, even that girl making that book on *Goldilocks and the Three Bears*, that's the retelling [of the story], but it's also picture-making

in the arts, and drawing three bowls of different sizes is mathematics [sequencing of size]. You have to look at it [the child's book] that way. Because of the five [curriculum] areas, it's all laid out separately in there [the document], but you [the teacher] have to make the connections.

Each classroom event, thus, like a child's retelling and illustration of an old story, contains multiple expectations. It is up to the teacher first to *see* all the expectations involved, to know how to communicate this to others, and to know what to do next to lead the child toward further understanding.

When I visited in April, Corrine commented that her board has offered an interpretation of the ministry expectations to teachers to assist in their struggle.[2] The document supports teachers in focusing not on individual expectations but on big ideas, such as the notion of uncovering, rather than covering curriculum, and of encouraging "enduring understandings" rather than rote memorization. Yet Corrine noted that it focuses on culminating performances and assessments rather than the emergent curriculum preferred in early childhood practice (Jones & Nimmo, 1994). However, the board apparently suggests that teachers focus on integration of curriculum: "I was just at a conference last week and teachers were saying, even if you integrate it, you probably can't cover it all, but you have no hope if you don't [integrate]." While Corrine thinks the documents "have some good ideas," she finds that all the specific expectations override in impact broader, more important curriculum goals. "[There's] so many of them, I think you lose some of that, the big ideas. . . . I think you have to look more at the overall expectations and not let yourself get bogged down with all those little specific ones. There's a better way of doing it."

What is this better way requiring integration of curriculum and synthesizing of expectations with rich classroom events? In April Corrine told me that she was going to teach first grade next year in order to "move forward" in her own thinking: she had been too lonely as the sole kindergarten teacher in the school and believed she needed interaction with a colleague.

I think people realize they *cannot* cover the curriculum unless it's integrated. . . .

So how would you do that? How would you make that synthesizing work?

Well you know what I'm going to do for Grade One? I'm going to photocopy all of the expectations in a different color for each curriculum area and I'm going to chop them up, and I'm going to

see what goes with what. What connects. The colors will help me
see how I can integrate expectations across the curriculum.

This kind of sorting is a well-used data analysis technique in qualitative
research methods (Kirby & McKenna, 1989; Miles & Huberman, 1984) and
a helpful process for synthesizing any mass of loose data. Corrine said,
"Well it's the only way I can work with it. I should have done this for kindergarten, but now I'm getting smarter. I'm figuring it out." She added in
her feedback that she is "figuring out how to better deal with so many
expectations—by looking for the 'big ideas' and connections across subject areas." The following September she said she had done the initial sort,
that it was "a bit overwhelming" but that she had found some "big ideas,"
such as a rationale for including a "Structures" program in first grade.

CONSTRAINTS, CHOICES, AND POSSIBILITIES

Constraints around Corrine's teaching arose from both the broader
school context and from institutional documentation requirements. Because
of her considerable responsibilities outside the classroom, as Primary Division Chair, her mental energy for thinking about her teaching was limited.
In addition, the program letter she was required to send home each term
outlining expectations and their assessment, while it might well have been
intended for the purpose of explicit, accountable communication with parents, nonetheless may lead teachers to regard the curriculum as their sole
frame of reference: how does a teacher think seriously about the development of friendship if the expectations omit it? Another constraint was
Corrine's sense that she had to assess all expectations for all children, although she found that children met different expectations in play. How was
she to resolve this tension? Overall, the greatest constraint for Corrine was
the fact that she was teaching a level for which she had no formal preparation and thus was learning about young children's development on the fly.

Yet she had made interesting choices to develop her teaching practice.
She was attracted by the exemplar of an experienced ECE colleague who
got her involved in an ECE professional development group. She altered
her teaching from the traditional toward the more developmentally appropriate in response, and developed skill in and commitment to pedagogical
documentation. She was changing her grade level because she was tired
of working in isolation and wanted interaction with a colleague. Her stance
toward the curriculum documents and board assessment checklists
changed from thinking they had to be done as given, to thinking of them

as guides. She also found the curriculum helpful in adding richer content (science and art in particular) to her program.

Corrine works both from children toward the curriculum documents and from the documents toward the children, reflecting her conflict over whether teacher-directed processes or developmentally appropriate practice should dominate her teaching. While the discussion about curriculum documents might give the impression that she works primarily from the documents to the children, this effect is contrived, I believe, by the focus of my research on how teachers in early childhood are taking up the new standardized curriculum documents. The examples of her work based in observation of the children's self-initiated activity, documented and displayed in narratives of photographs and texts, shows a capacity to listen carefully for what is going on in the activity of children, and to find ways to forge her own connections between meaningful events for children and the curriculum expectations that she must master in order to teach.

"I still look at the documents and try to make those links all the time"

Much of the work of this young teacher is forged around grasping what it is that children at her specific grade level are expected to know in a lockstep system, and in making connections between the abstract, semantic description of an expectation and the real-life classroom events in which those expectations are embedded. I suggest that the new curriculum expectations, set out in linear lists by subject area, demand highly developed abilities in teachers to synthesize and integrate curriculum on the one hand, and on the other, to differentiate and analyze the specific expectations layered into any rich classroom event for reporting purposes.

Corrine's teaching practice continues to develop in a developmentally appropriate direction, in spite of the press of board assessment checklists of subject-by-subject expectations. Her approach to the ministry expectations is one of investigation, exploring "what goes with what," in order to integrate curriculum. Her approach is also one of constantly forging links, working to build her own understanding of connections between events and layers of expectations. An interesting consequence of the new, more demanding and explicit curriculum is that it has paradoxically made the work of teachers such as Corrine more intellectually demanding. Especially interesting in Corrine's case is the extent to which she has absorbed a stance of developmental appropriateness, in spite of the lack of preparation in her background for teaching early childhood.

NOTES

1. Since the government cutbacks following 1995, my understanding is that in this board the reduced numbers of resource teachers have been concentrated in areas of special education.

2. In order to protect the confidentiality of the board, the document is not referenced or quoted from directly.

CHAPTER 4

Janet

The Resistance of a Developmentally Appropriate Teacher

If Grace was able to sustain a developmentally appropriate kindergarten, and Corrine was shuffling toward sustained appropriateness in spite of the new curriculum, Janet, teaching first grade, was not at all happy with the standardized curriculum. She disagreed with its appropriateness for young children, its superficiality, and its assessment practices. The conflict she perceived between her core values as a developmentally appropriate teacher and the direction of the standardized curriculum grew increasingly distressing to her as she watched her colleagues, who used to teach as she does, turn to worksheets, dittos, and what she considered to be excessive seatwork as the principal methods of teaching young children. Three compelling aspects of this conflict emerged in our discussions: Janet's sense of isolation within her school, her sense of alienation from the culture of teaching (so suddenly changed from what she knew it to be), and a conscious resistance to what she found to be disagreeable practices "not right" for young children. She had grown so disturbed by her experiences of the past several years that, as we began our research together, she told me she was trying to decide whether to stay in teaching.

Janet is a mature woman with 12 years' experience teaching kindergarten through second grade. She has a four-year degree in child study and early childhood education, a bachelor of education and a masters of education in special education. She worked for several years in child therapy before turning to teaching. She has, then, the sort of rich and varied background specific to early childhood education, in addition to a teaching credential, that the field hopes to see in teachers working with young children. Here is a portrait of an ECE-educated, experienced teacher distressed by recent changes, resisting those changes, wondering if the situation is tolerable for her. First I will provide an overview of Janet's classroom practices to illustrate a developmentally appropriate teacher at the first-grade level; then I will highlight her interpretation of the expectations, assessment, and report cards. Finally I will show her sense of being "under siege," her classroom a lone fortress of safety for her within her school. Could she tolerate such conflict for yet another year, and would she want to keep on teaching in such circumstances?

THE VIEW INTO JANET'S CLASSROOM

When I walk into Janet's first-grade classroom, she comes to chat with me, and the room of 21 children in full activity carries on without notice of us. The classroom appears to run itself (one of the paradoxical illusions set up by developmentally appropriate teachers). Three girls make elaborate bracelets and anklets at a cut-and-paste table, two tables of boys play at board games or games of their own invention, two children paint at an easel. A huge block construction winds across the carpet with half a dozen articulated spaces with colored papers and small colored blocks in arrangements inside: Janet tells me the girls have taken over the block center. The children are clearly very comfortable as they move about the room quietly, deeply engaged in their self-chosen activities. Janet tells me she keeps activity time as long as possible, integrating everything within it, but she has found she needs a separate writing time and, occasionally, a separate mathematics time. She incorporates much of the mathematics into activity time through homemade board games or through circle (large-group) time. I understand how the feeling of comfort and community is constructed when she tells me in September that she wants the children to feel that it is *their* classroom, that what matters initially is "relationships between kids" and "making the classroom a space for children: I want the kids to take over." She tells me, for instance, about a boy who painted a picture to decorate a particular wall, and how the children suggested a change in the way bins of materials were stored so there would be space to display their work. In other words, this is a classroom where power is shared with children, and children are invited to generate solutions to perceived problems. Simultaneously, Janet establishes clear limits: she tells me she has banned Pokémon from the classroom because she was unable to extend children's interest "beyond the desire to simply swap favorite cards." In another instance, when some girls brought nail polish to school with the intention of painting one another's nails, "It didn't go too far because I didn't let it." After she stopped them from using the nail polish, the girls measured, cut, and taped on construction paper fingernails, something Janet says she never would have thought of as an activity in nonstandard measurement. Janet thus assumes full responsibility for the life of the classroom but shares power with children when they are able to take some responsibility.

Observation of children's activity is important to Janet: she says it is by observing that she knows "what I need to do next." She speaks about the patience required to engage in an emergent curriculum: "You have to have those really, really sharp observation skills, and you have to be able to wait." She waits for something she "can really grab onto and run with." One of the sorts of things she watches for is meaningful events in the lives of young children that can be connected to school learning, such as important mathematics concepts:

> I try to make the curriculum relevant to the lives of the kids in my class. Instead of introducing data collection this fall by graphing types of footwear or hair color—common graphing lessons in Grade One—we graphed the different ways they have lost their teeth.

> After reading *Arthur's Loose Tooth* (Hoban, 1985) many children had
> a story to tell about losing their own teeth. Over the next few days
> we graphed this information and found that many children had lost
> a tooth when they were eating something. I can't do anything from
> a textbook that's unrelated to these kids and their lives.

Knowing she would be evaluating them on data collection for the November report card, Janet did this tooth survey with them, with each person having a slip of paper with one word to describe how they lost a tooth (e.g., fingers, toothbrush, apple, steak, chair). The slips were initially scattered randomly over the blackboard. Then Janet introduced how to organize them in categories and make a simple frequency chart: "We've also graphed pizza orders and library book exchanges." Janet supports children's choices, planning, and problem solving by observing and interacting with children throughout the long activity time, making connections between their activity and the literacy and numeracy requirements for first grade. She is able to see how everyday events in their lives become classroom curriculum that contains those requirements.

She supports children's play and child-initiated activity by, among other things, offering new materials to extend children's explorations, planning, and ideas, and also by suggesting other categories of activity for them. When she felt the boys were "stuck," for example, playing repeatedly with the same interlocking blocks in September and missing many other possibilities in the classroom, she invited them, in the afternoon, to choose a material they had not yet worked with, and they found the unit blocks.

What arises from such a curriculum is that the children are permitted, first, to generate their own ideas and to be creative—and this keeps them motivated to learn—and, second, to turn these ideas into real products in the world to share with others. The following excerpt from field notes shows the sorts of items the children create and the quality of their discussion together. On a day in April, at the group time at the end of the morning, several children were invited to show what they had made. Yarn had been added to the cut-and-paste table that day, and a boy had designed a small paper cutout figure attached to a long string, which he described to the group:

> "I made George of the Jungle, swinging."
> "Why," asks a girl, "don't you put them together [the two ends
> of the string] and then swing it [like a pulley]?"
> "How did you get the idea," asks Janet, "to make George of the
> Jungle?"
> "I just thought it."

A second child shows a kite with a long yarn tail.
Someone asks, "Could you take it outside to see if it fly [sic]?"
"When I was on my way to school, I was blown away!"
"Can you make a tissue one and fly it? Tissue flies really good."
"What makes it fly well?" asks Janet.
"It's flowy and it has a great kind of gravity."
Janet tells the children they can test out the kite idea with both tissue and construction paper.

Janet studies children's interests and knowledge, willing to integrate them into the "official curriculum" (the phrase is Dyson's, 1993), and struggles to understand and extend powerful interests of children that some teachers might not permit as part of the life of their classrooms. A group of boys, for example, became interested in a game they invented, sliding small constructions across the floor to see whose would go furthest. As the game evolved over several weeks, they understood that a smaller construction would go much further and eventually stopped making constructions and chose small plastic pieces from bins of material. Janet moved the boys into the hallway where their interest could be focused, and the boys, with exuberant joy and total engagement, would spend whatever time they were permitted (e.g., 30 minutes) shooting a little plastic cube or hexagon as far as they could, one after the other, from an agreed-upon starting line. They had their own rules and kept them fiercely: no throwing the piece, just sliding; use the starting line; shoot one at a time. It was like a reinvention of curling or golf, and these boys were ecstatically involved in informal physics, exploring the relationships among force, direction, speed, distance, and their personal power (Kamii & DeVries, 1993). This sort of activity remains stereotypically male, something parents and teachers have long noted seems to have little to do with enculturation and more with the fervent interest of males in speed, power, and projection. Janet was permitting them the invention and exploration of their game while also setting firm limits around their activity (no running to the end of the hall). Simultaneously, the day I spent time with the boys in the hallway, I noted the nonverbal disapproval of every other adult who passed by, implicit criticism in their posture and grim mouths, that such exuberant behavior was being tolerated in a school hallway.

Developmentally appropriate teachers are prepared to sustain complex and elaborate events designed and generated by children; to work with these events in ways that develop the symbol systems of the culture (literacy, numeracy) and the knowledge bases of the culture (science, art, social studies); and to keep school experience relevant to young children's experience of life (Bredekamp & Copple, 1997; Katz & Chard, 2000). Janet paradoxically sustains the patience to wait for children's ideas, plans, and problems to emerge, and simultaneously works at extending the boundaries of children's thinking. One of the ways she does this is by adding materials to extend curriculum possibilities and help children's thinking grow more complex. On the effect of adding material to the playdough table, she says:

> Well, we put beads out today, a dish of little crystal beads, and the kids have been using them to make faces and buttons on playdough people. I think for a few days they'll be experimenting, until they really start making plans and knowing what they can do with those materials, so it was more of an exploratory play today. After a few days I think they'll have more ideas about how to use the beads with the playdough in more complex ways, and watching what they do will tell me what else they might need at that center.

Another example of how she pushes the boundaries of children's thinking is her question to the boy who made the swinging cutout figure: "How did you get the idea to make George of the Jungle?" While he responds, "I just thought it"(and indeed subjective experience suggests that ideas seem to arrive in the mind fully formed), Janet nonetheless conveys with her question the notion that ideas have sources, a trajectory that can be traced, and lifts the discussion to the level of metacognitive awareness, of thinking about thinking, and about how one knows. Since an expectation on the third-grade assessment is that children can explicitly trace their thinking, Janet can be seen, by such spontaneous questions within contexts of personal meaning to the children, to be supporting the children's further development of a theory of mind (see Astington, 1993).

The previous description is not an exhaustive account of what makes a teacher developmentally appropriate but a presentation from the data (field notes and interview transcripts) intended to show the degree to which Janet is embedded in an early childhood framework for practice that emphasizes developmental appropriateness and an emergent curriculum.

JANET'S STANCE TOWARD THE STANDARDIZED CURRICULUM: DISPLEASURE AND RESISTANCE

What I hope to convey here is the overall sense of ethical dilemma that Janet conveyed to me in our interviews. Janet's perception is that normal classroom life has become threatened by a set of expectations and assessment requirements that she feels reduce and diminish her teaching so that it is made unpleasant and unworkable for her and her young children. Because of Janet's commitment to children, "to doing what is right for the kids," there is as well the sense of a potent moral and ethical dilemma for her, an implicit assumption that for her to give in to the changes the documents seem to suggest is morally wrong, for it might cause harm to some children. This interpretation is my inference as researcher, an argument that readers can assess for themselves as they read Janet's comments on the curriculum documents and new assessment practices.

Janet's View of the Expectations for First Grade

There are two threads in Janet's talk about the new curriculum expectations: one is that many of the expectations are as she would expect them to be for first grade; the second is that other expectations are "unbelievable" and "inappropriate" for this age. Here are examples from social studies, writing, and mathematics to illustrate these two threads of Janet's response. She says of social studies, for instance:

> One expectation is to know important past and present relationships in their life. And the example is with family members, friends, pets. So I have written down here, beside all those [general] expectations— every day, every day, every day that is happening in a Grade One classroom.

In writing, "two of the most important things for children to learn in Grade One are sound/symbol relationships and the spelling of some commonly used words, that's been a focus of Grade One teachers for years. There's a lot in the curriculum that teachers have always done." Yet she says, when she looks at the exemplars' guidelines for grading reading and writing (Ministry of Education and Training, 2000), that it is far beyond what Grade One children can be expected to do and is just not developmentally possible for many children:

> I look in the anchor papers we're supposed to refer to in grading— samples of A writing—that the ministry put out and the kids who get an A have to write at a level that I'm not sure I have ever seen before in Grade One. And the ministry's example of A level writing in Grade 8 reads like professional writing. I can't write like that, and I've been teaching for 12 years and I've got a graduate degree!

There is both disbelief and anger in her tone as she says this, conveying her interpretation that the exemplars are unreasonable, an A an impossible attainment for any child.

In Mathematics, Janet notes that in teaching the reading of time, teachers always taught time on the hour in first grade, but that most six-year-old children "just don't get" the minutes. The new curriculum adds the half-hour.

> When I sit down and work with the kids who are not "up to Ministry expectations" in telling time, I can get some to give correct answers by memorizing where the hands are at half past the hour, but when you ask them, you can see in their faces that they have absolutely no idea, there is no understanding. Even very confident children, they just don't get it.

The requirement of teaching something that she does not believe that children can grasp bothers Janet. Thus, Janet finds some of the content a "pushed down" (Elkind, 1990) academic content inappropriate to what she believes is reasonable development for children of this age.

Janet's second major complaint about the expectations is that they are too superficial, dealing with skills at the expense of deeper knowledge or values. "It's very superficial learning. Teachers frantically try to cover what they have to cover, knowing that it's a terrible way to teach." I had asked why teachers feel pressured to take up the curriculum in a linear, fragmented way, when nothing in the document directs teachers as to *how* the expectations are to be taught. She replies: "I think it's because it's so skills oriented and specific skills have traditionally been taught in a linear, fragmented way." When she read the first draft of this account, Janet added:

> When curriculum is taught in a systematic, linear way teachers can easily keep track and show evidence of what has been covered. There's a demand for children's learning to be observable and measurable. A stack of completed worksheets (or incomplete, as the case may be) is proof that a child has been "taught" certain concepts, even though they [sic] might not have learned them.

So the content is "covered," she finds, often at an overly fast pace that may in fact result in teaching that many children cannot follow.

In sum, Janet views the new curriculum expectations for first grade as too focused on simplistic skills rather than understanding, and thus too superficial, and in part inappropriate and unreasonable for children of the ages in first grade. Because of her interpretation of the document, she says she does not work with it very much.

Janet's View of Report Cards and Assessment

Janet tells me that since the expectations are end-of-year expectations, her principal "allowed" the first-grade team to choose their own three expectations for the November and Winter report cards for each subject area. The teachers on the first-grade team had to agree on and all use the same expectations. Janet says the only place she uses the curriculum document is to plan for the report cards: "We had to choose two or three specific expectations for each strand . . . and we had to make sure that we covered them in our program that term."

When I ask Janet how she works with the requirement of grading children A, B, C, or D in a developmental, meaning-centered classroom, she replies: "Well, that's the dilemma. I don't think it does fit. Most of what's happening in the classroom isn't reported on." Her interpretation, or her school's interpretation, of the reporting system is that the three specific expectations selected to be described on the report card are the only three expectations assessed for that area. Since the expectations are superficial and fragmented, and there may be literally a hundred in any one area of the curriculum, such as reading, writing, or mathematics, then only the tiniest fraction of the whole area is actually being reported on in the report card, compared to what is occurring in the classroom.

> And because every child has to be evaluated on the same thing, a child may be doing exceptionally well on something that is not being reported on in that term. Or a child may be having trouble in an area and that cannot be reported on, because it's not one of the expectations that were chosen [by the first-grade team].

In addition, since the expectations are changed for each report card, there's no possibility of showing improvement across the year, in Janet's interpretation, for that specific fragmented expectation, once reported on, is gone from the report. "If they make progress the next term, they can't get a comment on that progress because the expectations have changed. We have to go on to the next expectation." Janet says they choose the most global expectations, something most children can attain, and that she marks "humanely":

> We made an agreement we wouldn't give anyone less than a C, and we marked humanely. For example, if I was undecided between a B and a C, I would give a B. The grades are supposed to reflect achievement, not effort, but if a child put a great deal of effort into the task or demonstrated a great deal of growth I might give them a higher mark than the Ministry directs.

> *Was that accepted?*
> Nobody knew. We just kept it among ourselves.

She is also concerned that the emphasis has shifted from teaching children to classifying children by their grades.

> And you know that's another big push in the schools right now. It's all about sorting and classifying kids. We're supposed to be thinking about *rubrics* all the time. All the time! We're offered so many workshops on how to grade kids. And basically it's not really assessment. They're workshops about how to classify kids, how to sort them into A, B, C, D and to put that label on. And to prove their A-ness or B-ness or C-ness or D-ness.

Later, Janet wrote in comment on this, "These workshops are about teaching teachers how to label children, how to do a good job of something we shouldn't be doing to young children in the first place." My sense was that she found these workshops unethical.

Janet is caught in a difficult conflict in which her core values and experience lead her to teach following a holistic, organic framework, and the government-imposed assessment schema reflects a production model framework emphasizing technical skills. How does she respond to such conflict, and to the imposition of an approach to education in conflict with her background, values, and teaching experience?

A Teacher Under Siege

"Basically, I close my door. I do what I want to in my classroom." Janet's response has been to shut it out, wall it off, to shut her classroom door and carry on, and to permit the expectations and grading of reports to intrude only where it was impossible to avoid—three times a year. She conveys her resistance to the new curriculum in many ways throughout our conversations, interspersing her descriptions of what she does with remarks such as the following:

> It's September 24 and I haven't looked at it [the curriculum documents] yet.

> I don't rely on the expectations or the curriculum to plan my program. I'm running a program the way I have for 11 years; it's based on all my years of experience, my professional reading, attending workshops, courses I've taken—all my background experiences.

I can't say it [the document] affects my teaching because I ignore it, for the most part.

These comments should not be seen as willful blindness to a framework she does not believe in, but a self-protective fortification that allows Janet to continue teaching. While she prefers to shut out the expectations and assessment that are so problematic to her, there are visible instances where she has clearly made a modification to her teaching practice to accommodate what is required by the new assessment and reporting system. One such occasion occurred in mathematics, where she had to report on the extent of the children's counting capacity (by 2's, 5's, 10's, and so forth). Janet said she had to sit the children down with her to test them on that. A second instance was where she noted that the new arts curriculum described expectations in first grade on understanding qualities of line, and she had found interesting material at a workshop at a conference for working meaningfully with line with young children (Steele, 1998). In such ways, Janet shows us she is more permeable to the curriculum changes than her talk alone might suggest. Yet, as a researcher, I see a teacher who feels besieged, and who manages to keep on teaching by constructing a protected space within which she can function in ways she believes are in the best interests of young children.

Three aspects to Janet's sense of being under siege and need for self-protection to survive were present in the transcript data of our conversations. These three aspects are Janet's sense of isolation from her colleagues, her sense of alienation from a radically altered culture of teaching, and her conscious resistance to the 1997 curriculum documents and report card changes. Janet's conscious resistance can take the form of small acts of subversion. As an example, one day teachers found a set of pamphlets in their mailboxes from the Principal's Association that were to be inserted with report cards for parents:

> The pamphlet was written in support of the new report card, claiming that it provides parents with accurate information about their children's learning. It sounded like government propaganda. I thought the government wrote it. I can't imagine why the Principal's Association is supporting the grading of young children.

Janet was so appalled at the contents of the pamphlet that she asked if it was necessary to include it with the report cards. Told no, she not only left them out of her reports, but actively encouraged other teachers to refuse to send them out.

Janet suffers a strong experience of isolation within her school. She sees herself as a teacher resisting being swept into a superficial, rote way of teaching, and she is afraid that other teachers may have given in to the pressure to teach mechanically in spite of their early childhood values and beliefs about young children. She describes how photocopying of worksheets used to be done almost apologetically, but is now done openly, and that budgets for photocopying worksheets "keep going up and up." She laments:

> I don't know any other teachers in our school who are not worksheet teachers.
>
> In 11 years of teaching Kindergarten, Grade One and Grade Two, I haven't done a single math worksheet. And I'm not going to start using them now.

Since this change to photocopying multiple worksheets has occurred very rapidly, within a period of two years, there is, as well, for Janet, a profound sense of alienation from the work culture in which she successfully participated for almost a dozen years.

At our April interview, Janet in fact sounded so stressed that I commented that it was heartbreaking to see teachers such as her—among the more highly educated and experienced in the system—feeling so isolated and alienated. I commented:

> *The idea of people like you being lost to education is extremely worrisome because the knowledge and values you bring to the school are then lost from the culture [of schools].*
>
> The thing is that that knowledge is *not* valued. It is *not*, at all. I'm expected to embrace the curriculum, and I feel pressure to give my children more worksheets and homework and to run a teacher-centered program.
>
> And I feel as a teacher in the school totally unvalued.

To see the depth of Janet's sense of alienation, here is a comment from our April interview. Janet tells me that what they now receive from resource teachers in the board is merely information on assessment. "Packets, packets, packets on how to grade kids. People are abandoning what they know and believe!" I asked what would convince teachers to do that, when their beliefs might be different from what they felt they were asked to do.

> I just think there's tremendous pressure on people to go along
> with the curriculum—from the public, from the principal, super-
> intendents, parents. [pause] The EQAO test is a big thing, a huge
> amount of pressure comes there. I personally try to resist doing
> in my classroom what I believe is not in the best interests of my
> children, but it's often a very uncomfortable feeling to be doing
> this.

If Janet feels herself very much alone, this isolation and alienation have
occurred very rapidly, for she refers to herself and the first-grade team as
a "we" only a year earlier. She says when they were choosing the expectations that they would report on, their wish was:

> To do what's right for the children. That's what it all came down to
> last year when we were making these decisions. We kept reminding
> ourselves that we would do it the way that we believe is right for
> children. Not for administrators, not for the government, not for our
> colleagues [in higher grades]. We had to do what we believed was
> right for children in our classrooms.

Janet thus prioritizes the children and her knowledge as an early childhood
educator and does not accept that her knowledge and background should
be overridden by others who know less about children of this age. She is
unwilling to permit other interests to convince or compel her to set aside
this deep knowledge and conviction. In this, she appears to be somewhat
unusual, less compliant, and with a more developed critical perspective
than some of her colleagues. For a teacher such as Janet, in her insistence
on doing what she believes is "right" for children, there is not merely the
sense that her teaching life (and the learning of children) is being reduced
to something unpleasant and unworkable, but the belief that this reduction to skills and grading (classifying children A, B, C, or D) places her at
moral risk of harming children: she is not doing what she understands as
"right." Janet describes, for instance, a child she knows elsewhere in the
city who gets Cs and Ds because he has difficulty doing large amounts of
seatwork, describes how bright he is, and how unbearable he already finds
school by third grade. While Janet never explicitly stated that the curriculum was morally wrong—in its imposition of unreasonable requirements
and use of teaching methods that don't work well for young children—
this conclusion is tacitly present in her several passionate references to
"doing what is right" for children, and underlies her profound disagree-
ment and sense of alienation from her colleagues.

CONSTRAINTS, CHOICES, AND POSSIBILITIES

Janet feels coerced toward a simplistic form of teaching that she resists because it is, to her, morally unconscionable. She is distressed, emotionally upset, because to follow the changes in teaching in her school overturns her most closely held values about what matters with young children and how to support their learning and development. She has become isolated in her school as the only "holdout" doing child-centered teaching, and her principal does not understand ECE or offer her support. She frames her dilemma starkly as whether she should leave teaching or stay in conditions she finds intolerable.

It is perhaps not surprising that sometime in this 12th year, Janet made a decision to leave teaching. In addition to the ethical dimension tacitly present throughout our discussions and her refusal to do what she finds irresponsible, she experienced the new curriculum and grading practices as intellectually superficial and rigid. As an educated person, she wants to work where she has some independence, some space for her own ideas. Her sense of alienation from her colleagues, her sense of isolation and lack of support in the school, her conscious resistance as a strategy of a thinking person are all present in this comment of Janet's with which I close her chapter:

> There's no autonomy left in teaching. Teaching is becoming a non-thinking profession and I don't want to be a non-thinking person for the rest of my life.

CHAPTER 5

Ann

Literacy as the Focus of Curriculum

If I say that Ann is fairly typical of teachers of first grade, I mean that those of us close to teaching know many teachers who offer her pattern of interests and strengths. Her areas of greatest skill and interest are language, literacy, and ESL issues. Her strengths in language are accompanied by a capacity for dramatic story reading, an evident affection for young children, and a commitment to teaching and professional development. She was in midcareer during our research, with 15 years' experience, and typical in that her background was a bachelor of education from a local university. Such programs generally include no particular sensitizing to issues of early childhood education, and in fact Ann had expected to teach older children. Her knowledge of developmental understanding of young children, thus, was gained "on the job." Her commitment to teaching included continuing professional development: during our research, for example, she was enrolled in an ESL course that included action research in her classroom. During this year of teaching, half the "Stage One" ESL children in the five first-grade classes in her school were gathered together in her room. Her school board groups children into four stages by level of functioning in English, offering varying levels of support for each stage. Stage One referred to children trying to function in an English-speaking environment for the first time, during which they are often silent (Law & Eckes, 2000; Tabors, 1997; Viitaniemi, Bateman, Milne, & Shea, 1997). As I re-listen to the taped interviews with Ann, I am reminded of her sense of drama as she uses her voice—the crystal clarity of her diction, the precise inflection and careful choice of emphasis, the sense of pace that utilizes silence. It is the sound of a trained voice, self-aware, used as an instrument for particular intentions, a lovely voice and very easy to transcribe. I am reminded that this voice would be a clear, precise model of English for newcomers to the language.

How does Ann approach the new standardized curriculum? She attempted to honor it, to work with it carefully in conjunction with decisions made by the first-grade school team, and tolerated its frustrations, bringing to it a quality of teacher discernment that allowed her a sense of what to emphasize and what to omit, within parameters suggested by her school board. What we will see here is a view of Ann's classroom that shows the language emphasis, and some examples of how this plays out for the ESL children. Love of language, concern for affect, and a quality of challenging the children to do more—these are the themes in her teaching practice that I will highlight. First, Ann paid consistent attention to issues of language, frequently using books as a starting point for ideas for organizing curriculum. Second, she frequently worked to incorporate children's feelings into what they were asked to do, thus promoting some personal meaning in the technical focus of the curriculum. In other words, what she synthesized in curriculum decisions was a combination of the technical with motivation generated by children's feelings. Third, she challenged the children to do more by paying close attention to detail in the children's work and by not accepting what the children offered without pushing them to go beyond what they had done. These are three themes that I will highlight in this view of Ann's classroom. Then I will portray how she approached the expectations and the standardized reporting system.

THE VIEW INTO ANN'S CLASSROOM

As I entered her room on my second visit, I was thinking that this classroom looks "typical" for the urban area. How is it typical? The group of children is highly diverse: I see hairdos of cornrows, bobbles, Sikh head coverings. Physically, the classroom is typical in that it includes an open carpeted area where Ann sits in a rocking chair, children before her listening to a story. Adjacent to the carpet area is an area of tables and chairs for seatwork, lots of materials around the edges (a craft center "more for their imagination" in front of Ann's desk, a gerbil in a terrarium, layers of reading materials in a book rack that defines the backside of the carpeted area), and three layers of materials creeping up the walls. Children's paintings, snowmen collages, and many charts occupied the main level at blackboard height around the room. Above the blackboard was a frieze of numbers from 1 to 100 marching around two sides of the open area and off toward some cupboards. Above the number frieze were charts, one per month, describing who lost teeth that month. Near the entry to the classroom was a series of initial consonant alphabet cards with real objects attached, my favorite the item for "U," a set of large boxer shorts.

Literacy and Story Reading as the Foundation

The focus of Ann's program and of her motivation in constructing curriculum is books and reading to children:

> Now I could just read to them all day long. . . . I would like to read to them four or five times a day. . . . So much comes from books. I love reading books and you have their attention—they just love to listen. That's the most important thing at school—reading and listening to books.

In February, she is reading *Guess How Much I Love You* (McBratney, 1994) about "little nut brown hare and big nut brown hare." She read: *"I love you right up to the moon. Oh, that is very far."* The children laugh, enjoy the story, sit quietly, and are fully engaged as Ann reads with colorful expression and exquisite pauses for effect. When the story is finished, Ann asks,

> *What could you say to show you love someone? I'm going to make a list of these good words.*
> "High as the sky," says one child. Ann writes "high" on the flip chart. There are four or five hands up.
> "—low."
> *You'd have to make it really low to show how much you loved someone.*
> "—big," says someone.

"—universe."
What makes you say the universe?
"—across." The children's voices are so soft I can hardly hear them.
Any other ideas?
"As tall as a shark."
Is a shark tall? What's really tall?
"Water?"
Is water tall? Water is deep.
"Fat."
What's fat? Is water fat?
"An elephant."
"Long."
I love you as long as—?
"The school?" (This makes me smile, for the school is long and low, although it's hard to know if that is what the child intended. Does it mean that school lasts a very long time?)
"As a snake?"
We do think of a snake as long. Let's think of things we all know.
"High as the sky."
What's another word that means high?
"As high as the moon."
I'm looking for another word—
"Tall as a tree?"
Tall means high, doesn't it. It's going to be recess time. I'd like you to think of a little letter on [during] recess for someone you love.

She shows the children some pink hearts on which she has written several samples of the linguistic construction she wants them to attempt. One is for the gerbil, Rosie, and says, "I love you as deep as you can dig." Another is for her cat: "I love you as much as you can sleep." The sentences follow the pattern of the story read earlier. She tells them she has lots and lots of hearts for them to write on, more than 20, more than 30, at least three for each child.

After recess, the children return to the rug.

Did you do your recess homework? Did you think? She asks if anyone wants to share an idea.

A boy says of his brother, "I love you as much as you can cry."
Okay, now let's do that sentence again. Your brother's name is John?
Ann writes on the flip chart, "John," and says, *Why do I put a*

comma? Someone comments but I cannot hear. *That's not really the rule. What does the comma mean?*

"Pause."

Right. Pause for a second.

The boy dictates his sentence and she writes it. JOHN, I LOVE YOU AS MUCH AS—

"cry," says the boy.

You need some more English words. She repeats the sentence, adding *you can.* The class reads the sentence together.

Who's got another idea?

"Ma, I love you as long as you take care of me."

I'm going to change the words a little bit, so it doesn't sound as though you'll only love her as long as she cares for you. Ann writes: MA, I LOVE YOU AS LONG AS YOU HAVE TAKEN CARE OF ME.

When Ann read this account she noted that print doesn't show the way an affirmative tone or facial expression, such as smiling, offers encouragement to children: indeed, so much of the nonverbal aspect of communication is lost in print. There were 19 children in Ann's classroom, most of them children of color from many different countries of Asia and the Caribbean—Jamaica, Trinidad, Korea, India, China. Twelve of the children were officially designated for ESL support, four or five spoke English as their mother tongue, and the others "do speak some other language at home but aren't considered to be ESL anymore." The fact that many are Stage One children, just learning English, is somewhat apparent from their comments above, yet they participated with enthusiasm and interest, clearly attached to Ann and trying to understand what was asked of them.

When we discussed this lesson, Ann told me that she got the idea for having the children write little messages of loving "as much as—" from the book she read to them. Ann wanted to work on using language to make comparisons, to introduce the construction of a comparison to the ESL children, "but even the kids who do speak English completely, we're trying to work on some comparisons." It was close to Valentine's Day and Ann continued: "And it's about love. Just to get them thinking about who do you love? And how can you tell somebody how much you love them? It was really mostly to work on language. And they loved it." In this activity we see an exemplar of how Ann synthesized technical aspects of language learning—the functional use of comparisons—with the personal motivation of the children to express their affection for someone of importance to them. The children did indeed enjoy the activity and worked in an engaged way at the tables to write their message of love in relation to some large dimension or some activity the loved one preferred. The construction seemed sophisticated and conceptually complex for the children, a little puzzling. I overheard one boy at a table near me suddenly shout to his pal: "I love you as *big* as a killer whale. Now I get it! As big as a killer whale!"

Synthesizing Meaning and Expectations

I noticed Ann's tendency to link the technical demands of the standardized curriculum with personal emotional meaning for the children in several ways. One was the sort of activity above, where the teacher directly linked the children's personal affect with the requirement of writing a message, and tried to push forward the technical facility expected in their writing. A second instance of this sort of synthesis occurred in a mathematics lesson I observed in which the children were studying fractions. The children were trying to understand the notion of a half, and how to write ½. They didn't quite "get it."

> *I wonder if anyone can remember why we put the one over the two?*
> The children apparently don't remember.
> *What does the one mean?*
> "If you had a whole pizza and cut it in half."
> *Not quite.* The children don't grasp the use of the one and Ann explains that the one means one of two pieces: *The number on the bottom tells you how many pieces there are and the top says how many you've got.*

She had a worksheet for them with drawings of crackers, bread, and other foods to cut in half. But what motivated the children in this exercise was that they were to cut out and share each food item *fairly*, pretending it was to be divided with a friend. It was the notion of fairness, of creating two equal parts, that mobilized the children to cut and paste with care. One boy wanted to know whether he could write his friend's name on his portion. Again, Ann had drawn on the children's affect to ensure their engagement in a matter of fractions that, while part of the curriculum, seemed beyond some of the children both conceptually and linguistically.

A third example, where Ann couldn't see how to incorporate personal meaning and affect, confirmed my hunch that curriculum that did not have personal meaning for her and the children is very difficult for her to do. Within the science curriculum, the strand "Energy and Control," for example, did not interest her much. She commented that when the Science curriculum first came out, "none of us could find anything [resources], so we didn't teach it."[1] Energy is not a familiar area for Ann, and she has scant resources for it, but it is also unappealing to her: "Of course, I don't have a large interest in that area. It's a big joke among the Grade Ones [teachers]—'Ann doesn't want to do energy.' . . . There are no stories for me to read so I think it's a dry, boring unit." Without the drama of a character who reacts to things with feelings and responses, this teacher cannot find her own entry points to the curriculum. She inserts this love of personal reaction and of affect into the drier elements of the language and mathematics curriculum, but cannot as yet find adequate entry points for aspects of the science curriculum such as energy. Her way of bridging the skill-based curriculum and the children's current knowledge was to link it with personal feeling, either one's own feelings or that of a character in a story, so that the curriculum becomes linked with children's personal knowledge.

Ann's tendency to synthesize personal affect—what is meaningful in relationships—with the technicalities of curriculum expectations is consistent with her love of books and reading stories, and in fact shows why reading books was her highest priority. Storybooks contain characters who react to what happens: books combine personal affect and motivation with the drama of working out those desires and dilemmas. "My favorite times are when I'm reading to the kids. That's when, of course, they're best behaved and it's what I enjoy doing the most." I hypothesize that when the curriculum did not include people reacting with affect, it was more difficult for Ann to be sufficiently interested to be motivated to teach that content. I argue that this tacit understanding of how to make the dry, technical curriculum appealing is an essential feature of her teaching practice. I would also point out that she is absolutely accurate in her judgment that young children cannot learn where they have no personal meaning invested, and that neurosurgeons and cognitive scientists such as Damasio (1994) have demonstrated the close workings of affective regions with the thinking areas of the brain in rational decision making.

Language as the Prod to Attend to Detail

Ann's teaching style was one of teacher direction in a rhythm of stories and instructions given to the group at the carpet interspersed with pencil-and-paper tasks at tables. While the children were expected to accomplish the specific activity, the atmosphere of the room was relaxed and comfortable: there was always someone moving around to sharpen a pencil or find some necessary tool. Often there was a line to see Ann during the time children were working at tables, each in turn having a miniconference with her. Generally the result was a return to one's place to work on some aspect in more detail.

   The following episode shows how she demanded more from the children than they originally thought to put into their work. The children were working on bird research on this day, drawing an illustration of the bird that their group was researching. Each group used a photograph as a set of reference points for their drawing. One group drew a hen, one a penguin, a woodpecker, a blue jay, and so forth. Here are excerpts from my field notes of Ann's interactions as she circulated among the tables of children drawing.

> One boy has drawn a bird about an inch long on his 8 ½ x 11 paper. Ann says: *I think that's too small. It's really hard to see the head.*
>   The child turns his paper over and starts again. As she passes the penguin table, Ann suggests that the children outline their bird in black so the white portions will show better on the page. To someone else, she says: *Check the feet in the book.*
>   "Oh! *Black* feet." The child colors the feet black for two seconds and takes the page to show Ann, who has gone elsewhere.
>   *Look at how black those feet are [in the book]. Very black. Are yours very black?*
>   "No." The child sits down and colors more. Three seconds later he is up and off to show her again.
>   *I see a big long beak on the penguin. I don't see a long beak on yours.*

When we discussed this episode I commented on how Ann pushed the children to notice more. She called it paying attention to "detail": "Just pointing out the blue jay's head, it's not really round like you've drawn it, what do you see? 'Oh that pointy part, okay.'" Piaget, among others, noted that intellectual development is a matter of increasing differentiation (Crain, 1994). Certainly even the commonsense view suggests that to get better at doing something, one learns to see (i.e., differentiate) more and to use what has been noticed in more elaborate ways. When we admire the work of a dancer, an engineer, a musician, a surgeon, an actor, or the worker who uses an excavator with a feather touch, it is in part because they show us an impeccable precision, an articulation of detail that we had not imagined possible. In the case of Ann's insistence that the children notice more and attempt to notate it in their drawings, we can recognize the attempt to prod them to go beyond too simplistic a rendering, to notice more about their world and react to it. Her comments gave them examples of where they might look further and what more might be perceived.
   The development of writing is closely interwoven with drawing (Dyson, 1988, 1993; Ferrario, 1984; Steele, 1998) and closely linked to children's understanding that writing is a symbol system that represents

speech (Vygotsky, 1976). When drawing, children represent visual images in two-dimensional symbols, while in writing they represent images of sound in two-dimensional symbols. Both forms of symbolization are abstract notations for three-dimensional sensory experiences. I speculate that Ann's work on the children's bird drawings—which she may have thought of as science—was probably equally important to the children's grasp of the symbolic nature of what you are asked to notate on paper in school.

ANN'S STANCE TOWARD THE STANDARDIZED CURRICULUM

Ann's approach to the first-grade curriculum expectations and reporting system had two interwoven aspects—her dominant, preferred way of working with them and a secondary, less preferred approach. Her dominant approach was to keep a close focus on the selected, targeted expectations by subject area: I call this a linear, segmented approach. Her secondary approach was to design units that integrated curriculum across several subject areas. I will try to show how both aspects were present in her teaching and also that her emphasis was on a more focused, segmented approach.

A Linear, Segmented Approach

The first-grade curriculum has 380 expectations divided into five subject areas—Language (60), Mathematics (106), Science and Technology (107), The Arts (57), and Social Studies (50). Ann, together with the other four teachers of first-grade classes in this school, chose about three expectations per subject from the curriculum documents for each term that would serve as their targeted focus for the report card. My understanding is that three expectations in particular are targeted because that is the amount of space for reporting on the report card, although more than those are taught. Because Ann felt the curriculum to be so massive that it was impossible to focus intentionally on all of it, she and her colleagues understood that they had the principal and school board's support to choose what they believed most important to emphasize in their teaching. (This approach was taken in three of the six schools in my research.)

> We as a team look at the curriculum, and we try to decide what's the most important, which of these outcomes in there really are the most important ones. Where can you do the good teaching? Where can we really get things across?

But, of course, teachers must teach more than the three targeted expectations for the report card. When Ann describes what she was attending to in an activity, we can see how several expectations were nested or layered into one activity. Ann described the writing activity of sending messages of love on the pink hearts in such terms:

> The point of the writing activity was to try and give them some vocabulary, and whenever I'm writing on the chart I'm working on spelling, although I didn't focus on that today. . . . Previously they've learned that a sentence has a capital, a sentence has a period. That was coming out. . . . And it was about writing a message, a little mini-letter, and then they learn "as much as."

Later, she adds that the basic concern is whether the writing conveys a message, "does it basically make sense." The nested expectations thus are to convey a coherent message, to grasp an English construction for making a comparison, to use conventional sentence structure, spelling, and punctuation. Yet she had also said, separately, that it was about love and "telling how much you love someone."

The selection of the most important expectations, in the view of Ann's team, and working with these in "packages" that keep the focus segmented by subject area, thus determined for Ann the actual content for many classroom events. Yet within this segmented, linear approach to curriculum, with a nesting of three or four subject area expectations within one activity, was a less dominant approach of integrated units. Ann commented that integration of curriculum was expected: "I integrate whenever I can." She used "mapping communities" as an example to explain this to me.

> Okay, like the mapping communities social studies unit dealt with a number of expectations in the Social Studies curriculum, but the book I chose to read had to do with a character going on a trip and the pathway followed. Some of the language outcomes can be dealt with because I'm also getting them to write a story about that character. So then, I could work on periods and capitals. While we were mapping, the children had to measure, so you're pulling math in. They had to record that; whenever they're recording, they're working on writing expectations.

When I asked Ann which approach she prefers, she said, "I think that's a personality thing with teachers, and I like to package things so that I know the parameters of it." In my first draft of this chapter, I thus saw Ann as a teacher who preferred a clear set of boundaries within which to function.

I inferred from this that she preferred to keep subject areas reasonably intact, and speculated that this preference for a segmented-by-subject approach is one way that teachers who have not had ECE background might differ from those who have. Ann disagreed with my interpretation, arguing as follows:

> When I say I like to package things I mean that I like to know what theme (package) I'm working on (i.e., birds) and then I have a base from which to pull in other areas. However, some themes like "place value" need to be taught as a set of lessons to be learned properly. They can't be evaluated properly if one place value lesson was hidden in the Bird theme and another hidden in the Mapping Unit, so for some things I do use a "linear" approach, when I think it will help the children.

I think part of the difficulty could be that the curriculum places understanding of technical skills (like grasp of place value) on the same level as broad issues such as understanding animals, that the linear list makes no distinction in value of one skill in relation to other understandings or knowledge. She also saw herself as having ECE background because her teaching had been in kindergarten through second grade, whereas I was referring to having access to a particular field of study with its own literature, values, and sets of teaching practices.

Rubrics as Levels of Achievement of Linear Expectations

Ann now uses rubrics to move from the expectations enclosed in classroom events toward grades on the report cards. While the commonsense notion of a rubric is that it is the criteria by which the expectation is judged, Ann's description of the rubrics she used suggested that the system imposed by the government in 1997 has generated a simplified, formulaic, or mechanistic standard set out in terms of crude quantities. "The rubric is one sentence that you change for each [grade]—A, B, C, or D. The B comment is usually the expectation. We expect a B."

Grades are distinguished from one another by a set of "qualifiers," words agreed upon by the team to separate children into the four categories. In describing how Ann evaluated children when using a calculator to explore number patterns, Ann said the team used four different "qualifiers" for A, B, C, or D.

> The B is the met expectation, using the qualifier "often." The A might be "consistently shows evidence of understanding when

using a calculator to explore number patterns." A C is usually a child who needs help. And D is "rarely." . . . A child who gets D just didn't get it.

I infer that for Ann, the term "rubric" now refers not to a complex criteria, but to the four "qualifiers" used to describe *how* the child works with regard to the expectation. A rubric, for Ann, means "how" to categorize for four grade levels. The qualifiers tend to be chosen to reflect quantities (*rarely, sometimes, often, always*) or accuracy or independence (*needs assistance, does it alone*).

The B level, as mentioned, refers to mastery of the expectation, such as being able to put periods on the end of sentences. I am puzzled then as to what an A would be for such an expectation. Ann added here, "In many cases, so are we! This is a question we often ask."

And that's often the most difficult part. So usually we take the B, and then we go C, D, and then we go back up to A [in devising qualifiers]. So often we need to stick in "consistently" and "confidently." "Creativity," we'll stick in that for an A.

It is unclear to me how a first-grade child could be creative with periods. If meeting the expectation earns a B on the report card, then A is for doing more, for exceptional performance. But if you have mastered use of periods, what more can be expected, unless perhaps you are an established poet? Teachers are left, thus, attempting to invent some difference in skill between a grade of A and one of B, where there is scant discernible difference for basic skills. It would appear that the government's reporting system conflates a competency-based system (linear lists of mechanical, skill-based, technical outcomes or expectations that everyone can achieve) with a comparative system that *ranks* by merit.

Elsewhere Ann complained that "we're pigeonholing these kids" when they shouldn't be, and "how hard it is to fit some of these kids into our rubrics." I asked Ann if she thought the report cards showed what the children know and can do. She said, not like the reports that she used to write, in which she described the children's accomplishments anecdotally. She said of children who go beyond what is expected, "There are always those kids who can do that, but we're not really supposed to report on that; we're supposed to report on what the curriculum says." Thus what is reported to parents will be what the child can do in relation to the curriculum, not what the child has in fact learned or accomplished. Many have written about the problems of standardized curricula reducing teachers and children to a "lowest common denominator" (e.g., Wien

& Dudley-Marling, 1998). In Ann's comments we see how teachers can become coerced into thinking up four gradations of value for simple technical expectations, like using periods conventionally. I worry that such coercion reduces the field of teachers' vision, so that they might become unable to see larger goals, like communicating ideas succinctly or telling a story. I worry that because they are so busy assessing the children's relationship to the curriculum, teachers could become unable to see anything beyond it as important.

Ann's Evaluation of the Standardized Curriculum

When I asked Ann how she thought her teaching had changed since the standardized curriculum was imposed in 1997, her discussion indicated that in some ways she finds the curriculum improved and in some ways she finds it has made teaching more difficult. "I think a lot of teachers have been forced to teach more science." As we have heard, for teachers of Ann's temperament, books and story reading and interest in language issues are the passionate roots by which they make the curriculum come alive for children: if they cannot find the story of a character that feels and reacts to inject into the curriculum, it becomes difficult to invest their commitment. Nonetheless, Ann found the attention to science a positive change—"for the better." A second change "for the better," she thought, was the way it directed teacher attention: "I think it has really focused people, where maybe some people were floundering before, or doing . . . stuff [just] because they liked it." She pointed out that the standardized curriculum thus directed the teacher's agenda in ways it previously did not, and she found that direction helpful.

On the negative side, Ann commented several times on how the joy and life had gone out of her teaching. "The negative side, that we as Grade One teachers seem to chat about, is how it just doesn't seem fun anymore. It's not fun for us, and it's not as much fun for the kids." When I asked Ann, *so what makes it not fun*, she made two main points: "We are moving away from things we've done that don't cover things on the curriculum, but we know from experience these are important skills for the children. . . . Things we used to love to do, like more around Valentine's Day." My inference is that these omitted events have strong social components. The standardized curriculum is more focused on individual attainment of academic skills than on pro-social processes of friendship, community, relationality, citizenship, or democracy (Portelli & Solomon, 2001).

Her second complaint concerned the massiveness of the curriculum: "The curriculum has too much in it. That's our main complaint. We don't have time. We don't have time. We keep saying that. And we're throwing things at the kids so fast they don't have time to learn them properly."

In addition to the positive comments about the curriculum leading to more focused teaching and more science, and the negative comments of massiveness and its omission of areas important for young children's development, there were other comments in our discussions that revealed further problems with the assessment and reporting system now required by the government. Ann commented on the terrific tension for teachers of young children between sustaining a sense of developmental understanding and the assessment requirements. "We have so much trouble with the wording of the curriculum and applying it to these little developing beings. And then further, we're asked to give them a D, or a C, or a B or A. Which just about kills us."

When we talked about the massiveness of the curriculum, Ann said: "We have been struggling with this [its size] ever since this curriculum came out. We kept beating ourselves up. We'd be tearing our hair out, so frustrated. . . . Some of them [children] just aren't there, they aren't developmentally ready for this curriculum. They are just not." She made the comment that academic material "got pushed down" into earlier grades and conveyed a sentiment I have heard multiple times from teachers in this urban area: "We're convinced that the people that did some of that decision making were not educators. They couldn't have been!"

Ann also commented that while the expectations are written as "end-of-year expectations," the curriculum is so massive that she and her team were assessing end-of-year expectations even in first term. She commented also that once an assessment had been completed, for instance children's understanding of time (perhaps in February or March), there wasn't time to return to it to see whether children who hadn't understood it then might have by year's end. For this teacher, end-of-year expectations meant that all during the year, the list of expectations was taken up in a linear way, simply to attempt to get through them.

At one point Ann suggested that children's natural rhythm or learning pace is very different from the pace of the standardized curriculum organized like a production schedule. Ann was describing how "slow" some of her children were in terms of time necessary to complete activities. "I'm at a point now where I have some kids that are so critically slow they don't finish anything. And if I don't give them time to finish it, then it's already a C, because once you have to help them with something it's not a B anymore. That's the way our rubrics are written." The speed the curriculum suggests to this teacher, in its massiveness, thus works against the developmentally appropriate pace of the child's time frame. Ann is forced into a production schedule model of time organization that she recognizes reduces her children's chances for success.

Overall, Ann felt that the cumulative problems in the way she (and by inference, many other teachers) was using the curriculum resulted in a curriculum that was, oddly enough, not standardized at all. Because of the choices the teachers made as to which expectations would be emphasized, teachers could be working on very different areas within a subject. "When [the government] tells people that these are common report cards, we laugh. Because they are not. They are so subjective, subjective in that my school is reporting on this, another school on [something else]." These new report cards, she said, were actually easier to write than the ones she formerly composed, because the only thing that changes from report to report within a classroom is the "qualifier" that describes the grade. "It's cut and paste on the report card." Ann said the result is a report card that sounds "stilted." "But we keep being told [by the school board] this is what the parents wanted. When they complain, you remind them that they voted this government in, and this is what they wanted."

Ann thus takes up the standardized curriculum with close attention to expectations by subject area, using primarily a linear, segmented approach. She is frustrated by the massiveness of the curriculum. That massiveness results in choices by teachers of targeted expectations that may lead to a less standardized curriculum. The massiveness also results in Ann's understanding that she teaches faster and less thoroughly at times, and evaluates end-of-year expectations long before the end of the year. In these respects a linear, segmented approach seems to work not only against the rhythms of children's development but also against the government's overall intention.

CONSTRAINTS, CHOICES, AND POSSIBILITIES

"It's the report card that's driving this." Ann interprets the standardized curriculum and reporting system as a literal prescription for what she should do, a map that shapes and regulates her teaching and reporting practices. The tacit choice that she makes is to accept this prescription and follow its regulatory impact as best she can, though she sees grave difficulties for her and the children. I speculate that the choices she makes are unconscious because she feels locked into a linear, segmented approach to teaching and does not, at this time, see other possibilities. She has also made, in my interpretation, a tacit choice to link affect as much as possible with the technical tasks of the curriculum in order to motivate children to care about these tasks. Consciously, she continues to emphasize her passion for books, reading, and language as the vehicle by which to motivate herself. She accepts the standardized curriculum and reporting system, but she is not happy about it.

NOTE

1. One week during the first year after the Science Curriculum was published, schools received notice they were to order, within a week, $10,000 of materials and equipment, or they would lose the money. With an impossible timeline and only catalogues of lists from which to order, teachers in many schools had little input into the decisions of what to purchase.

CHAPTER 6

Susan

A Classroom On-Task

Susan is a strong exemplar of the public's notion of a traditional teacher, one who keeps the children marshaled to the school agenda, and who does so while consistently demonstrating care for the children. At the time of this research, Susan had 9 years of teaching experience and a background of a B.Ed. with an undergraduate degree in psychology. Because of the shortage of teaching positions when she graduated, Susan spent 4 years in supply teaching and long-term occasional positions. She did not, in fact, have her own classroom until 1995, two years before the standardized curriculum was imposed in this area. In this portrayal, thus, we see an example of how a teacher's practice has developed in response to the curriculum when she did not have a long history prior to it. Her B.Ed. included no particular sensitizing to issues of early childhood education or developmentally appropriate practice, although she had some familiarity with a day care program and had taught kindergarten for her school board. Susan happened, by chance, to be in the same school as Ann, the only school in which I did not meet the principal. In her classroom, Susan came across as having the sort of intense and powerful personality that motivates others, sweeping children up to follow her agenda. She also had a disposition of conscientious support for the children, one that leaves "no stone unturned" in efforts to educate them.

Susan's 20 children in a first-grade classroom were typical for this urban area in that they were highly diverse, their families originating from locations such as Pakistan, Vietnam, India, the islands of the Caribbean, and Ecuador: 4 children in the class were white and 16 were children of color. For much of the year, however, only two children were considered ESL learners, and even they were Stage Three (i.e., requiring monitoring but no formal support).

THE VIEW INTO SUSAN'S CLASSROOM

Susan's room had something of the ambience of dressage, with its tremendous skill, discipline, and intensity of focus. Dressage (meaning "to train") is the tradition of horsemanship in which rider and horse, in close partnership in a small ring, perform a series of increasingly challenging maneuvers. Riders guide their horses with highly differentiated signals and compete to be the best. Moves and obedience of the horse are judged: a head toss or tail swish can be considered resistance and points can be deducted. In Susan's classroom, the teacher's agenda, the standardized curriculum, was ever-present—like the maneuvers in dressage—the children gently but firmly held to the task of its performance. Throughout my visits, Susan kept the children on-task and motivated to the agenda of the curriculum, which was carried out largely as a pencil-and-paper experience.

The effectiveness of this on-task motivation was confirmed for me by the fact that the children paid no attention to me during my visits. I knew they had been prepared for my presence among them by the stage whisper of one boy as I walked in, "She's here." Once there were two men in coveralls who noisily entered the room and proceeded to repair a heater behind a vent in the wall adjacent to where Susan was teaching. Aside from scant glances in their direction, the children took no notice of their presence or activity, and indeed, within a minute the men had quieted down and went about their investigation in whispers. Susan quickly and irrevocably established who had authority within the room, and the fact that what had authority was the standardized curriculum and her role as keeper of the curriculum.

The ways in which a teacher structures her performance to accomplish her intentions is highly complex: what I will highlight in this chapter is but a portion of these structures. I will show how four aspects of Susan's teaching practice—her handling of time, detail, shaping of behavior, and affect—contributed to the disciplined feel of her room: it was the interaction of these that constructed the ambience and intensity of dressage. While the dressagelike feel, using conventional teaching, was the dominant form of teaching practice in Susan's classroom, there were also signs of a less dominant practice that included early childhood values, and these will be described. Where these two frameworks for practice intersected, an intriguing conflict occurred between organization of time and organization of space. How does she address the conflict?

Susan's Preferred Practice: Conventional Teaching

When I examine my field notes from Susan's classroom, four qualities stand out repeatedly. The four aspects concern (1) Susan's handling of time frames, (2) her close attention to details of the curriculum, (3) her continuous shaping of children's behavior, and (4) the use of her own affect to motivate the children. She used brief time frames, switching uses of time with maximum efficiency. While there were many transitions, they were brief, smooth, and economical. Second, she paid continual close attention to details of the curriculum. In language, for instance, in the midst of reading or doing word games, she noted which words were compound, the adding of "S" for the plural, the use of the apostrophe or comma. Third, in her carefully crafted language to the children she continually made explicit exactly what she wanted the children to do, as in, "If you sit cross-legged, the lap board will balance very well." Last, she continually let the children know the degree of her pleasure or displeasure with their compliance with this shaping, as in, "I'm not really happy that we have to wait," or "I'm a little disappointed: you need to be looking at the words [while you listen in reading group]." The interaction effect of these four elements within the flow of classroom life is illustrated by excerpts from several time frames, followed by additional examples of these strategies.

On one visit I arrive during reading groups. When the reading groups end, the children are called to the rug, and within 30 seconds, a child is reading out loud to the group. He is "guest reader" for the day, and reads from a book he has chosen and practiced. Recess at 10:20 interrupts the reading. Fifteen minutes later, the boy picks up where he stopped. As he reads, Susan puts drawings of signs of spring the children did the previous day after a walk outside at each of their places at the tables. The reader reads "beauty button" and Susan goes to the rug area and says, "Can you try that word again?" B-E-L-Y. He gets it. "You're reading really well," says Susan. The reader is sent to pass out writing journals at each place at the tables, while Susan chats with the children about yesterday's walk.

How did the clover look when you picked it up?
"It was still growing."
The leaves were folded shut. What did we find at the back of the yard?
"Moss."
"Garbage."
"Snow."
When you go to your tables, you will see your pictures. In your journal, I'd like you to write about our spring walk. What did we see?

11:00 A.M. The writing is laborious for the children: they form the letters slowly, looking up from their work, erasing, changing pencils, sitting chin in hand or leaning on an elbow. Sometimes they look back through their writing journals, or simply sit, running a hand through their hair. Then another word goes down on the page. Susan moves around the tables, chatting and responding to conventions of writing. One child wrote, "I went to a walk." Susan explained, *"We say 'for a walk.' I'm going to ask you to change that."* To another child, *"Great, you've got your period [at the end of the sentence]."* To a child writing about finding balls, *"Ball or balls?"* To another, *"Is it geen or green grass?"* She acts as monitor to their work, pointing out small errors. She also compliments and shapes behavior. *"You're on your second page. Good for you!"* *"Table One, there is far too much chitchat. Mark, please turn your chair around properly. Thank you."*

After 15 minutes, she sits at her desk, and the children line up to see her. In red pen, she corrects their writing. Susan tells one boy that he needs to watch his finger spaces between words, that his words are hard to read. *"Good ideas, though."* His writing says:

We went on a spring walk. We saw green gras garbig mub [and] clover Robins, [and] buds iris. It was fun.

Susan adds commas in red after grass, garbage, and mud, writes "Good!" and puts a bumblebee sticker in the corner. She talks to him about how to use commas with a list and places a sticky note saying "finger spaces" on the cover of the journal. He goes to the puzzle shelf and chooses a box, but Susan tells him he won't have time to finish it, to work on his "I can read" book instead.

The chatting of two boys at a table nearby is distracting her and she tells them to *"be quieter,"* they're not working *"in their head."* Their chatter continues and she quickly responds, *"Douglas and Jahar, go to yellow, please."* The boys jump up, go to a chart, pick their names written on Popsicle sticks out of a basket, and place the sticks in a yellow envelope on the chart.

At 11:27, six children read books of their choice in the reading area, and most children are finished with the writing task, as Susan calls the group to the carpet. She goes over the instructions for "Mad Minutes," a worksheet for addition problems done as a power test. "Mad Minutes" lasts 15 minutes, 12 minutes for going over the instructions for the test (this is one of the first occasions that the children used this kind of worksheet), and 3 minutes for the test itself. Instructions include such comments as:

> If you have a question, a quiet hand will bring me to your table.

> If you make a mistake, it's all right to cross it out. Don't use your eraser, it's too slow.

> How many can you do in a minute?

As I sit, I am thinking how power tests, assessing how fast something can be done to a timed deadline, mimic the contexts both of standardized testing and industrial production schedules for manufacturing.

After lunch, Susan works with the Word Wall for 10 minutes, examining the new words—*new, make, I'm, them*. Then she announces, "Instead of starting with DEAR [drop everything and read], I'm going to start with a calculator job, then DEAR afterwards." The calculator job is a worksheet test on number patterns, skip counting. The children are to do three patterns, coloring their results in three colors on the hundreds chart on the worksheet. If they are counting by 5, for example, the calculator provides the increments by 5 and they count along the sheet and color in the square with that numeral. They are to work alone, as she will be testing other children in using the calculators and won't be available to them. Going over instructions occupies 10 minutes, and the test itself is completed by most children in another 10 minutes. Then they read self-selected books as Susan continues to check individual children's use of the calculator at her desk.

Taut Time Frames. Most activities that I witnessed spanned 15 to 20 minutes, often in a rhythm of 15 minutes of instruction followed by 15 minutes of work time. The children, thus, were trained to expect a change in agenda roughly every 15 to 30 minutes. Susan kept them on-task during the time frame and no time was lost in transitions, as transitions lasted the time it took to move from the rug to their places at the tables. The quick transitions occurred because of Susan's careful organization: she laid out the children's pictures, for instance, as the reader read, and the reader laid out the children's writing journals as Susan chatted with the children, reviving their memories of the walk. If one imagines time as a net, the spaces in the net of time in Susan's class were small, the net itself thick, the net held taut to the task of the curriculum. Time was held taut, like a spring.

Close Attention to Details of the Curriculum. We see in Susan's comments to the children as they wrote in their journals how she attended to the small details of conventional writing so emphasized by this particular standardized language curriculum. While Susan acknowledged the children's good ideas, what she emphasized was the details of conventional writing that the standardized curriculum described in its multiple lists, as in: "We say 'go for a walk.' I'm going to ask you to change that." "Geen grass or green grass?"

What puzzled me was why the children's ideas for their writing were all the same, and why the little drawings to place-hold their memories were all in precisely the same location on the six squares of their papers. In my first draft of this chapter, I asked why the children were using identical sets of reference points. Susan responded that they had walked together, and as someone noticed a sign of spring, they all stopped and drew a visual reminder in the next square. The expectation that Susan attended to states that children "describe seasonal changes." When I asked what a child would do if she had her own ideas about what to write concerning the walk, Susan responded that she finds that "Writers at this age need an idea to spark their imagination." In Susan's responses to my first draft, I saw that the set of reference points had been constructed collectively, an activity done in unison, so that each child would have sufficient content to write about "signs of spring."

Continuous Shaping of Children's Behavior. Susan "nips in the bud" any signs of wandering from the assigned curriculum task. For instance, toward the end of a 15-minute group session on clock time, highlighting "A.M." and "P.M.," one boy began to finger some blocks on a shelf beside him: "Take your hand from the blocks. Turn your body," was Susan's immediate response. He did so, his expression suggesting discomfiture. A child whose sweater fell to the floor was told to put it in his backpack in the hall; she'd already spoken to them about excess clothing yesterday. A girl who put the pink hood of her pullover over her head while writing attracted Susan's comment: "We don't wear hats or hoods in school. Take that off your head." My field notes for visits of several hours duration contain 6 to 12 such corrections for each visit. These corrections to the children were always positively phrased and explicitly worded: like a signal on the horse's rein, the child was told precisely what to do.

Use of Affect to Motivate Children. While time frames were a taut net to hold children to the curriculum, and close attention was given both to details of the curriculum and to shaping children's behavior to attend only to the curriculum, there was a strong sense of positive accord toward the children, a prizing of the good work they were doing. Susan frequently commented "Good!" or "Good job!" to the children as they worked. When I commented, "You're really conscious of telling them when they've done a good job," she said how important it was to "genuinely mean it. You have to genuinely deliver it because they're very perceptive." Susan also showed great courtesy toward the children, thanking them when they responded to her requests, making all her comments in a firm but even tone, a matter-of-fact tone. It was clear that the children wanted very much to please Susan, because they responded to any request or individual correction with alacrity. Although I witnessed no misbehavior, Susan said sometimes she might ask a child to sit apart from the others as a consequence of a misbehavior. Her most severe correction had been to leave a boy sitting out of the activity time, but that was quite unusual. Her comments to the children consistently told them how she felt about something, and also goaded them to be their best. Here is a further sampling of such comments:

> Brent, can you get the clock under the wall? Thank you. We're getting very good at telling time.
>
> It would be nice if you decorated the borders with crayons.
>
> Can you [a group of girls] make an effort not to be silly? I'm going to check with the lunch monitor and I hope to hear good things about you.
>
> Table 5, go open your calculators. And I know you're going to do your best to get back to wonderful.

That Susan developed close attachments to children in her classroom was confirmed for me when I accompanied her on yard duty and observed her checking whether one boy had mittens today, whether someone else was coming to chess club Tuesday, and then watched children flutter over to chat with her, Susan telling me how nice it was to see children she had taught in previous years.

Less Dominant Practice: Aspects of Early Childhood Education

While the four aspects highlighted in the above view of Susan's classroom comprised dominant aspects of her teaching practice to this observer, such a view of Susan holding children to the standardized curriculum is one-sided and does not acknowledge aspects of her practice that were attuned to developmentally appropriate practice. Two aspects in particular were clearly evident. One was the value placed on meaningful, hands-on activity as a basis for learning. The second was attempting to provide some child choice and child pace in activity.

Meaningful Activity. Ensuring the meaningfulness of assigned tasks was important to Susan, and evident, for example, in the walk in search of signs of spring, and then the drawing of pictures to place-hold them in memory before attempting to write in their journals. Susan said she did this "because I thought it would help them with their writing, . . . I think it gives them something to work from." One ESL child did not write about the walk, but about her teddy bear; "I wanted to support her in that." Yet Susan also notes that "She's usually better at following directions." A second example of how Susan attempted to keep technical aspects of the curriculum meaningful was the way she attached the lesson on "A.M. and P.M." to activities that the children would do at specific times, inviting their ideas about dreaming, sleepwalking, and falling out of bed during the night hours.

Attempting to Provide Choice. The second aspect, providing for children's choice and pace of activity, was evident in Susan's careful child-centered organization of space. Susan's design of this normal-sized room included many developmentally appropriate activity centers laid out in small, roomlike arrangements. An art area with an easel and sandbox was adjacent to a little science room with a low table backed with a display of bird photographs and some handmade bird feeders. An interesting mathematics area with many structural materials for construction, lots of puzzles, and math board games also contained a computer center at one end. The reading center overflowed with many kinds of materials, from basal reader series to handmade pattern books that acknowledged every member of the class, and a writing center with mailboxes was nearby. All of these areas were in addition to the table and chairs area for seatwork and the carpeted area for gathering together. Susan clearly enjoyed composing and providing for these areas, telling me, "I wanted to have a science table this year. . . . We're doing electricity next so I'd like to change it to an electricity table with lots of batteries and bulbs: it's more of a hands-on [area]. I try to change it on a monthly basis." She also commented, during another visit:

> It's really nice to have a sandbox. It's a water table too sometimes. But for measurement, for volume, with sand or water, it's very valuable. They enjoy going [there]. The dramatic play yesterday between Donny and Jim at the sand table, you know, it was great— the dinosaurs were there, the bulldozers, the tractors. I know they're from different time eras, but . . .

The five activity centers were used by the children during the last half-hour of the day, the children organized into groups by table seating and assigned a particular center for each day of the week. Susan also used this half-hour to squeeze in individual reading conferences of 10 minutes each with three children. Thus genuine choice was circumscribed both by organization of groups, daily assignment to a center, and by reading conferences, but the idea of choice was retained.

Interaction of Meaningful Activity and Child Choice. The interaction of several practices together contributes to particular directions in a classroom. Occasionally, the expectation of meaningful activity and of limited choice resulted in children shifting outside the time frames of the curriculum production schedule. On one occasion, a boy who had completed his main task during a time frame went, rather than to the second required task, to the science area to work on his bird research and the completion of a blue jay out of plasticene. He was there when I arrived in the room, and told me, as he stacked two blue balls of plasticene, adding black lines over the eyes, that

> "Blue jays are the meanest bird. They trick other birds."
> *How do they trick them?*
> "They call like other birds. They can do fifty calls."

He then made black feet with toes to fasten onto the body.

Another child had researched woodpeckers on a CD-ROM nature encyclopedia by himself and found out, as Susan described: "Woodpeckers have really long tongues and we had seen in videos how it's got little barbs at the end to hook the insects, but he found out how the tongue is so long that when it retracts its tongue, it actually wraps around the inside of its skull." She told me this as an instance of how children "love getting the facts, they like to know that," and how important it is to "teach them how to gather, and be information gatherers."

While these aspects of early childhood practice—an insistence on personal meaning for children, and organization of space to promote child choice, planning, and pace in activity—were present in Susan's classroom, they were contained within brief time frames that remained a minor portion of the overall time-on-task nature of her teaching.

The Conflict of Early Childhood Organization of Space and the Production Schedule

The conflict in Susan's organization of space and time was to encapsulate the values of early childhood education in organizing space and the values of a traditional school production schedule in organizing time. Early childhood organization of space suggests expansive uses of time (following the natural rhythms of children's self-selected activity) and organization of materials and resources into centers or spatial areas as the dominant means by which one offers curriculum (seen as interesting things to do and think about). Location *in space* determines different activities. School organization of time as a production schedule establishes curriculum as instruction, and location *in time* determines changes in activity. How did Susan work out this tension?

The location where these contradictory practices intersected was in the reduction of use of the early childhood spaces to one brief time frame, like any other subject of the curriculum. Since the "subject" of activity centers is the child controlling her own agenda, making decisions about what to do, what to think, what to plan, initiate, generate, and complete, the importance of these values to Susan can be seen in the fact that she finds a time framework in which to honor them, in spite of a curriculum that focuses on linear expectations.

However, in the face of the standardized curriculum and her own conscientiousness, the production schedule and the teacher's agenda to support children's mastery of the curriculum dominated. For example, early in the year she had permitted children to go to their assigned center once their primary task was completed during other time frames in the day. But she had stopped that process: "I'm trying to get away from the free activity time after an activity [assigned task] because I find that too many kids rush through their work." She now has a second assigned task that the children can move on to when their main activity for the time frame is completed. She described how if the children were writing they would now take their time, but "if they know they can go to the construction center and build after they're done, then I'm not going to get more than one page from some of them. And I want to avoid that." The centers, thus, which so predominate in the spatial organization, are used but during one-tenth of the scheduled school time, because in schools organization of time dominates organization of space. I make the inference that Susan cannot see how the curriculum for which she feels so responsible might be embedded in the centers.

While the space was organized to suggest many activities occurring simultaneously with some child choice and setting of pace, in the style of classrooms that follow frameworks for early childhood education, it was the organization of time that actually determined what Susan and the children did. Time as a production schedule, following the industrial model, is typical of most Western schooling, with scheduled fixed time periods in which to produce specified outcomes or products. This production schedule organization of time is, to me, the most taken-for-granted aspect of Western schooling—that is, the assumption that what is normal is the organizing of events in a linear line, one after the other through days, weeks, months, and years. Elsewhere I have called it the "train curriculum" (Wien & Dudley-Marling, 1998). We have lost the conception that there are other ways to use time in learning. It does not occur to us unless we experience powerful exemplars of different handlings of time, such as aboriginal views of time as circular (Royal Commission on Aboriginal Peoples, 1996; Sheridan, 1998) or agrarian views of time as cyclical, such as in the approach of the early childhood educators of Reggio Emilia (Edwards, Gandini, & Forman, 1998). Until we experience other models of organizing time, we don't grasp that organizations of time are cultural inventions.

But if Susan was solely interested in the production of the curriculum in the children, there was no reason for her to go to the trouble of including the many engaging activity centers in her room. Is it possible that Susan's organization of time and space serves as an important exemplar of what has been occurring to early childhood practices in the primary years? Standardized curricula, written in linear, fragmented lists, presuppose production schedule organizations of time, space, and materials. Such curricula may lead teachers to override early childhood organizations of time and space. In Susan's case, her organization of time was shaped by the habits of schools and by the linear organization of the curriculum, and her organization of space was shaped by early childhood values. Susan wants those early childhood centers as part of her program, though the press of the curriculum has removed her capacity to observe and work with them, since she conducts reading conferences when the children are in activity centers. When she read this comment, Susan added, "They *were* more a part of my program. I [used to] run my program through centers half the day. It's been two years since I've done that. I've changed because of the new curriculum. I hope to return to a center-based program."

How will she will work out this contradictory tension as she continues teaching? Will the centers gradually disappear under the duress of the imposed curriculum? Will the centers expand across time frames to incorporate the standardized curriculum? In what direction will Susan's teaching preferences and the pressures of her teaching context lead her?

SUSAN'S STANCE TOWARD THE STANDARDIZED CURRICULUM: LINEAR AND SEGMENTED

"You start with the curriculum and you look at the expectations and you work backward from them." Susan takes up the standardized curriculum in a linear, segmented design, attempting to pay close attention to the specific detailed and technical expectations for each subject area that the curriculum documents contain. Under the press of the massive curriculum, she crafts brief time frames, using each one for specific tasks connected to each expectation. That time rushes on, changing the task to something else, was occasionally noted by these first-grade children. Once a boy called out, "I didn't get to do this." Susan replied, "Tomorrow is another day." Five qualities of her linear, segmented approach for teaching and assessment follow.

Differentiation Increases the Quantity of Expectations

To show an example of the massiveness of the curriculum, let's use Susan's comments on Mathematics, which in first grade traditionally concerned number sense and the understanding of quantities. In the current standardized curriculum, mathematics has five separate strands, each to be covered every term. The five strands are, as described by Susan, "number sense and numeration, then measurement, then geometry and spatial sense, patterning and algebra, data management and probability." Susan commented that the first-grade team did four of the strands during the winter term: "We were going to do all five this term but it was too much. We wanted to spend more time on adding and subtracting, so we eliminated one [strand]. Number patterning and algebra will be commented on [the report card] next term." Susan commented that trying to cram so much in made her "more aware of time—time limits," that she is conscious of having to finish things quickly. "I'm more blocked into time frames," thinking that areas have to be taught, that is "covered" in, say, "two weeks."

Piecework Assessment

Workers in the garment industry in the early 20th century were paid for piecework, for instance, how many sleeves they sewed to standard within a set time frame (Apple, 1979; Giroux, Penna, & Pinar, 1981). The linear, segmented approach to the standardized curriculum suggests the same stress for teachers and children in trying to learn set content within a teacher-prescribed time limit. The time limit is necessary in order to assess the material, so teachers can be held "accountable," as Susan said, to parents. There are so many expectations that teachers cannot realistically assess them all at the end of the year. In a linear, segmented approach, the expectations are assessed when they are "covered." As in Ann's situation, this means that end-of-year expectations are assessed throughout the year, whenever that particular curriculum content is undertaken. It also means that teachers cannot go back to reassess expectations that specific children might have missed at the time they were undertaken, because another new expectation demands to be addressed.

> I can't go back and reevaluate and say, their mark is improving now because they understand it –
>> *Because it won't be on the report card third term?*
> Because that was second term. You understand what I'm saying?

Here is an example of how the reality of piecework assessment worked for Susan in mathematics. Her school had informed parents that what was assessed in the fall term was not necessarily assessed again in the winter or spring. In other words, there isn't an opportunity to get better at something. The child gets it when it's "covered," or credit for "getting it" is lost.

> We let them [parents] know, particularly in math, that what we're evaluating first term is not necessarily what we're evaluating second term. So when someone gets an A– for data management, let's say sorting in first term, and second term we're assessing graphing and their ability to collect and interpret information from a graph, it bothers me when I'm doing a report because I see, oh, they got a B– this time, and that's going to set off some alarm bells [in parents].

Susan complained that parents think the child is not doing as well, when in fact the assessment is of a different field in mathematics. If there used to be a cumulative sense in subjects such as mathematics, that sense of doing better is apparently lost in the increasing differentiation of the curriculum. In addition, the child's pace of learning is overruled in a production schedule. Susan said of the end-of-year assessments occurring throughout the year, "And I don't feel comfortable with it."

Tension Between the Production Schedule and Children's Development

I had the impression that although Susan worked intensely to teach the curriculum, there was underneath the surface of her teaching deep tension for her between the linear, segmented approach that she undertook, and her sense of the children's development. When she commented on time limits and how she felt she was blocked into time frames for covering curriculum, she said she "didn't like it. Because I don't feel like I'm really considering where they are, what they're ready for, because according to my plans I need to talk about [for instance] number patterns right now." Another example concerned teaching the children to tell time:

I wanted to be fair to them, and we needed more time with the a.m. and p.m. and I wanted to do a lot of follow-up on it. So it's my second week [on it]. We haven't been doing it every single day, but I feel that they need some more time, . . . but I'm aware that I have time limits to work with.

Assessment as Triangulation of Evidence

Susan did not like testing first-grade children, and said she used other processes. She worked with three forms of assessing children's understanding and achievement—collections of sample work, observations and anecdotal notes, and individual conferences with children. "I can't evaluate through pen and pencil." In teaching the concept of clock time, she might have worksheets as samples where the children have drawn in the hands of the clock at various times. She has also been "watching them and taking notes" when they are working with a partner and a wooden clock to simulate different times on the clock. "How I really feel comfortable in Grade One is doing a lot of my testing through conferencing." The conference is a personal interview in which the children show Susan what they know and what they can do. In watching these conferences on my visits, it appeared that the children enjoyed these moments of having the teacher to themselves; they appeared to be brief but intimate interludes after which the children felt good: she encouraged them all.

An aspect of discomfiture for Susan regarding the assessment was the demand to give first-grade children a grade of A, B, C, or D and to justify it.

> What's an A? Why did they get a B in that? A lot of it comes back to evidence. I can specifically say, "Well, here is what they did." When I began [supply] teaching there was a little developmental continuum, and it was "beginning to develop, is developing, well-developed." You just moved the little arrow. Well, things have changed.

How have they changed? Susan must cover material "in more detail, and more breadth and depth" and justify her selection of grades with evidence, so she is accountable.

> Although people aren't questioning me, I always feel that I need to justify and prove [the grade I give]. I'm more accountable.
> *Do you give D's to your kids?*
> I did first term. Some who, you know, weren't reading, weren't writing, no comprehension of letter names, let alone letter sounds. But not this term. I have a really hard time. It's really hard to give a Grade One a D. How do you do that when you're trying to build them up and make them feel positive?

Threads of Holistic Responsiveness

Yet the linear, segmented approach to curriculum did not override all processes of assessing children's functioning in Susan's classroom. In addition to the activity centers at the end of the day, and the importance of research in science, and Susan's emphasis on making the curriculum meaningful to young children, her approach to the teaching of writing showed a holistic responsiveness. We did not discuss every area of the curriculum, and the reader might extrapolate from Susan's comments about teaching writing and grasp that there is much more going on in her teaching than surface attention to details of the curriculum. When Susan describes working with the teaching of writing, we see the layers of concerns she thinks about simultaneously and how the details are nested within more holistic processes, such as the *invitation* to respond. In working on expectations in writing, she might be working simultaneously on children's ideas, on moving from simple to more complex sentence structures, on use of capitals and periods, and on small steps or "interim goals" adapted to individual children.

> Like writing, I'm looking at their sentence structure. Are their ideas, are their sentence structures complex? Are they simple? . . . Are they including lots of different ideas? Now I didn't specifically encourage that they write complex sentences [today], but that's one of the things I'm looking for. Now another time, I might model that in the whole group [instruction time]. . . . We talked about how to use commas, and I encourage it in a very suggestive way and see if they implement it.

We gain here the sense that many aspects of writing occur to Susan simultaneously, some large and some small, that she *invites* the children to attempt certain aspects and *waits to see* the children's responses to these invitations. A disposition to invite and watch for response suggests the presence of reciprocal responsiveness, an aspect of holistic practice that is ruled out of prescriptive production schedule ways of doing things by design (Franklin, 1999). Yet it is present here. We thus see examples of how dispositions to work more holistically are present under the surface of the thrust of a linear approach to the standardized curriculum.

CONSTRAINTS, CHOICES, AND POSSIBILITIES

Susan felt that her teaching had become more segmented than it used to be, more fragmented into discrete small time frames, and that she was "teaching in chunks" and it "wasn't as holistic as it used to be." Like Ann, she felt that this curriculum had removed a lot of the pleasure from teaching and learning: "We feel as though we've taken a lot of fun out of learning." She is very constrained by the standardized curriculum, taking it on the whole as a literal prescription for teaching expectation by expectation in a linear, segmented way. Susan also told me that at the end of each school year, she is so drained that it takes her a month to recover. "Physically I'm exhausted. Physically, I'm exhausted. I'm mentally drained. I'm not sleeping well, I'm not eating well. And then by the middle of the summer I'm feeling okay. And slowly, I start gearing up to go back."

Susan lamented that she wanted to work in a much more integrated way. She commented that she believed "teaching *had to be* more integrated." Susan's lament, that she wants to work in more integrated ways, ways that keep some fun in learning, leads me to this interpretation of her teaching practice. Susan has not had the benefit of an education background that could illuminate for her how to work in more integrated, holistic ways: such a background can be gained from several sources. These sources include developmentally appropriate pedagogies such as emergent curriculum

(Jones et al., 2001), project approaches (Katz & Chard, 2000), holistic approaches such as the approach of the early childhood educators of Reggio Emilia, interpretations of Reggio Emilia in other countries (Sweden, Canada, United States), approaches such as Gardner's multiple intelligences (1999) or brain-based education (Caine & Caine, 1997), all of which provide sophisticated alternatives to the linear, segmented production schedule. Susan herself was hoping the school board could offer more support in coping with the curriculum in ways that would integrate it more fruitfully for life in classrooms.

Because Susan is superbly competent, she makes the production schedule in a linear, segmented approach work for her first-grade class. Yet it leaves her exhausted and drained, and the long-term effects on the children are not clear. There are sufficient signals in Susan's teaching—her organization of space, her comments on how she teaches writing, her persistent desire for meaning in children's work, her support for children's own research—that suggest that her dominant practice in teaching was a response to the linear, segmented design of the curriculum documents themselves, and that the shaping of her production schedule is derived from the format of the documents. In my first draft, I said I was unsure whether her teaching at the moment of our research together was an accurate reflection of how she wanted to teach: she replied, "It's not how I want to teach, but how I feel I must, for now."

CHAPTER 7

Ellen and Penny

Tension Between Meaningful Experiences and Pressure from the Standardized Curriculum

Ellen and Penny teach second-grade children, gap-toothed 7-year olds. Each teacher has a class of 24, but they work in a double classroom in which the adjoining wall is removed. They team-teach in that they plan collaboratively, coordinate their activities and, while often remaining with their own classes on separate sides of the room, also join groups for activities such as sketching animals in a local wildlife park or making three-dimensional animal habitats in class. Teaching is public work often done in private, behind a closed door (K. Krupnick, personal conversation, Harvard Graduate School of Education, Winter 1989). Ellen and Penny have overcome the problem of teacher isolation, and collaborate to try out ideas, plan, and discuss challenges: they are in continuous contact even when working across the room from each other. How are these two teachers taking up the new curriculum?

Ellen and Penny are both mature women with considerable experience. Penny has been teaching for 12 years, 5 of them in second grade. In her first five years, she taught special education classes at several levels and also first grade. Her B.Ed. credential includes a 2-year specialization in special education; Penny has strong developmental understanding, in addition to particularized knowledge of difficulties in learning. Ellen's B.Ed. required a credential in early childhood education as a prerequisite, in addition to a university degree, so she has strong understanding of young children's development and knowledge of the research base underlying pedagogies recommended for young children. Ellen came to teaching in midcareer, having worked for decades in social services in Canada, Australia, Thailand, and Indonesia. Ellen thus brings to teaching an unusual breadth of knowledge and personal experience, as well as maturity. It was Ellen's first experience teaching second grade after teaching a year of kindergarten and a year with a first-grade/second-grade split. Both teachers bring a depth of specialized knowledge and understanding to their teaching.

Ellen and Penny confront and attempt to resolve the tension of two conflicting commitments: they are committed both to honoring the standardized curriculum expectations and also to honoring their values about teaching young children. They had made, thus, a solid commitment to covering what they experienced as a huge curriculum, with many strands in many subject areas. Yet, with their strong background in developmental understanding of young children, they believed that second grade learning must be hands-on, relevant to young children's lives, exciting or "fun," and respectful of individual differences. While these two commitments themselves may not seem contradictory, the intersection of two separate knowledge bases and sets of values creates conflict for them. As pointed out in previous chapters, these conflicting values arise from contrasting frameworks for learning—the production model that sees learning as incremental, cumulative, and pieced together (like a machine in an assembly line) and the holistic framework that sees learning as interwoven with organic processes of growth and development, of relationship and socialization, with all things interconnected (Davis & Sumara, 1997; Filippini, 1997). These teachers, too, had become sites within which such conflicts are engaged. How will the conflict be confronted and resolved, or can it?

Ellen and Penny, in addition to this difficult conflict, were also tolerating, in the year of our research together, some annoying systemic constraints of space, time, and materials that should be recognized from the outset. The school had lost half its library and its computer lab to make space for classes brought inside the school building from portable classrooms that could no longer be used because of mold. Although the computers were distributed among individual classrooms, only a quarter of them could be used because of setup and wiring problems. As well, funding cutbacks to school boards meant that teachers had to supervise lunch hour. Two classes in addition to their own ate lunch in Ellen's and Penny's classrooms, so that table space to display work or leave out projects under way was nonexistent: every available surface was used for lunch for 90 students. The teachers' personal lunch hour was reduced to 40 minutes in length, something they noted was barely time to eat, make telephone calls, and use the bathroom. I mention these systemic constraints to demonstrate how the working lives of teachers are pinched, so that less is reasonably possible and everything creative has to occur in a context in which time and space are totally filled with scheduled things to do, and resources are reduced.

THE VIEW INTO ELLEN AND PENNY'S CLASSROOMS

Following recess on a day in April, the two groups have just returned from a concert in which they performed songs about recycling. Today this final hour is composed of a long activity time with children working on several different projects, and a 15-minute group time before dismissal.

On Ellen's side of the room, three children at a table with notepads and books engage in research on the Arctic. Some children work on texture designs, using rubbings made outdoors (the fence, bark, concrete, etc.) and cutting out shapes from the various textures to compose a picture. Nine or ten children sit at the arts table working with plasticene to represent their newfound understanding of Arctic life. They make fishing holes in the ice beside hooded figures with tools in hand, or figures wearing anoraks, or fire pits and igloos, and one boy makes a polar bear and a white fox.

On Penny's side the children are all working at tables on various projects, some on story posters; some on science experiments or transformational geometry, tracing shapes in a design that rotates them through all possible permutations; and some on writing stories. The class has studied a painting of a hockey game (*Hockey* by Henri Masson, 1940), and a number of children are writing stories about the painting or about hockey. One girl is constructing pop-up hockey figures for the cover of her book. At group time I stay on Penny's side and listen as children share their work. A boy reads a story he wrote about a fisherman, a long story that includes illustrations and a math problem involving numbers of fish caught (39, 57, 17), later all correctly tallied in the story. Then Penny shows a new book, pointing out its gorgeous endpapers and illustrations. She invites a girl to show the book she is making and comments on the design of her endpapers. Penny notes several other children's plans for their books, conveying a sense of looking forward to their completed projects. The child making the pop-up hockey players on her book cover shows the class her construction, and Penny holds it up for all to see. The figures are impressive because they are easily recognized as hockey players, and because of the sophisticated colors and agility of construction, for they pop up and lay flat with ease.

While I was visiting Ellen and Penny's classes, the children appeared comfortable, relaxed, and evidently enjoying whatever activities were under way. There was always lots going on, and the children were attentive to it. Nevertheless, Ellen and Penny's conversation with me in our interviews showed considerable tension, tensions they continuously confronted and attempted to surmount.

ELLEN AND PENNY'S STANCE TOWARD THE STANDARDIZED CURRICULUM: TENSIONS

Appeasing the Curriculum

The problem for Ellen and Penny was the struggle to unite their understanding of how young children learn with the tremendous pressure to cover the demands of the curriculum. There are, in the second-grade curriculum, 83 end-of-year overall expectations and 380 specific expectations, with five separate strands in Mathematics, five in the new Science and Technology curriculum, a new Social Studies curriculum, and a new Arts curriculum, all to be incorporated in addition to the important expectations for Language Arts. The impact on these teachers of having to think about so many separate expectations for content, skills development, and understanding in children is that they continuously feel pressure to move on to the next thing. The pressure to cover curriculum content means that teachers control how time is spent in the classroom, such as when activities stop and start. As in Susan's case, the pressure to include more content results in shorter time periods for individual activities, thus increasing the intensity of uses of time. Samples from interview transcripts will show their experience of this pressure:

Penny: We really have to make sure we get through all the Science, all the Social Studies, to make sure all the areas are dealt with. We really do a lot every day. I used to have more time to do creative writing, time to read. I didn't worry if I didn't do Science every day: we only had to do 3 units a year [of Science], so you could really get into them in depth.

She describes how if someone brought a nest to show now, he or she would have merely 2 minutes to show it and then they would have to return to the scheduled lesson.

Penny: I just find it's more cramped. . . . We just get started on something, just get into it, and then in order to be ready for something 3 days from now, we have to stop, keep switching, and that's one of the most frustrating things for me, switching gears. It takes them forever because they're not into [switching to something else].
Ellen: No, no, and they're not in control of it [time] either, and they have no power [of choice] around it. *We* have all the power.

One hears in this lament on being pulled into specific uses of time, such as short time spans for activities and frequent transition, the early childhood teacher's concern that locations of power are no longer shared with children, but are totally controlled by the teachers. Because child-initiated activity and some valid child choice of what to do is seen as fundamentally important to the developing child (Bredekamp & Copple, 1997; Genishi, 1992; Jones & Reynolds, 1992), teachers who understand this research but who feel coerced by a curriculum to control time fully experience tension and struggle. Ellen thought it difficult to share power with children in such circumstances. Here is another example of how this tension emerges.

Ellen: To do a good job means to teach every little tiny expectation, and there are hundreds. I think that's the expectation placed on us!
Penny: —and make it meaningful! And manage to get to it all, too!

They speak about the pressure of too much to do, and the harassment of frequently interrupted work. During my second visit, for instance, the children had 15 minutes to work on their designs and constructions of a piece of model playground equipment (an activity generated from the Science strand on structures and simple machines).

Ellen: We're always finding chunks of time, instead of spending a whole morning or afternoon on it, which would be far better.
Penny: We struggle with that every day. . . . They've got all these things to do, and they're clamoring to do them, but we just get at them, and [say,] "I'm so sorry, but you have to tidy up." It's very frustrating because they're always being interrupted.

Total teacher control of time, a consequence of pressure to cover a demanding curriculum, nonetheless goes against the grain for these teachers because it destroys qualities of learning experiences that they value, such as sharing power in choosing some activities, responding to children's own pace in learning, and permitting children to follow their own excitement and passion in learning. The following three examples will show how this pressure is present in their work.

When Ellen's children were making plasticene representations of arctic scenes, Ellen commented that this work on the Arctic was driven by their desire to understand more. It had nothing to do with "any expectation in grade two: . . . This is spontaneous and this is unusual, because in this short period of time, we need really to cover more than we are." She implies that this is not "legitimate" activity, but rather time "stolen" from the curriculum, which has more authority than the teacher's judgment about her children. Although Ellen is able to override that authority, its presence is continuously felt.

Another example occurred one day after recess. Ellen was besieged with a litany of complaints as the children settled on the rug before being sent to work.

I have a tummy ache.
I have a headache.
I have a backache.
Oh and I hurt my head!

The children's complaints came fast and furious, and it was clear as they chatted with Ellen and several went to rest at their seats that the children were visibly relaxing as they described their sore body parts. I commented to Ellen later that it seemed as though the children required that relaxed space to unwind a bit, that they were not able to move directly into the next teacher-selected purpose. I interpreted the event as a request for a pause, a few moments of "breathing out" (Jones & Reynolds, 1992) before taking up the momentum of performing according to the teacher's wishes. Ellen commented:

> But you know, the whole time that was happening—and I value that time, part of me, my training and everything else helped me understand how valuable that time is—but the whole time I'm thinking, this is 2 minutes being taken away from activities, this is 4 minutes, 6 minutes gone.

Again we see time in schools conceived as a moving train, and one catches or loses it. Ellen understands children's more varied paces, but is caught in the conflict of being the arbiter of time on curriculum.

But this press to move along the curriculum train has consequences for more than intensity of experience. It also affects content. Ellen spoke of how, in their study of animals in the fall, many children showed excitement and motivation to study individual animals (cheetahs, bats, whales, spiders, a stick bug), but it was difficult to offer time for this, because the curriculum required that they learn about *categories* of animals, definitions of amphibians, reptiles, mammals, and so forth.

> We have to cover a huge amount just in life systems in animals in Grade Two. We can't let them just take off with an interest they have because we wouldn't be able to collect the data that we need to evaluate. . . . If they are independently researching a mammal, for instance, they can't spend a long time researching that mammal, because they're going to miss the information they need about reptiles, amphibians, birds, the rest of it.

In sum, then, qualities of learning contexts that are highly valued in the early childhood field, such as some genuine choices in activity, child pace in learning, and following the children's lead in pursuing their interests and passions as emergent curriculum (Genishi, 1992; Jones & Nimmo, 1994; Wien, 2000), are in conflict with the teachers' commitment to a demanding curriculum and fear they cannot do the curriculum or the children justice without giving in to the pressure to move quickly and intensely.

While the pressure of the fast-moving curriculum train was most visible in teachers' perceptions, it was difficult to assess its impact on the children. The children appeared comfortable, relaxed, confident, and enthusiastic. The affection and support of both teachers for the children was obvious, and the classrooms did not *feel* pressured. The children in general did not show symptoms of distress, although the sore tummy and headaches might suggest stress, a moment of brief resistance to the curriculum train.

On one occasion, a 15-minute period to work on design and construction of the model pieces of playground equipment was clearly too short, for the children had just begun when they had to stop. The danger of switching activities so frequently is that it may teach children that what you are doing doesn't matter much, since it will change in a few minutes anyway. And the necessity of being prepared to switch gears means that deep engagement and sustained activity become impossible. One issue of real concern to teachers is whether such curriculum pressure to cover quantities of material harms or even destroys children's concentration span by never providing the opportunity to sustain activity.

When Ellen provided feedback to me on this chapter, she added, in commenting on time problems, that "it is impossible to adequately provide one-on-one attention for the purposes of re-teaching, reviewing and re-framing in order to enhance understanding, within the time frame of this curriculum." One important tension that Ellen and Penny struggle with, thus, is the press to cover curriculum content and "attain" the expectations versus the press to honor values in educating young children of permitting some child choice, some child-initiated activity (such as the research into cheetahs and bats), some learning at a child's individual pace, and some expressions of personal interest and excitement in learning.

Teaching Expectations They Believe Are Developmentally Inappropriate

A second tension for Ellen and Penny is the struggle to deal with some expectations for the end of second grade that they believed were unreasonable for children of this age and level of development. For example, in social studies, children are expected to know hemispheres, continents, oceans, and the Equator in second grade. Ellen and Penny work with these requirements every day by having the children find places on the "where in the world map." Ellen comments that she finds aspects of these requirements inappropriate, for instance, grasping a concept of the Equator, and I ask, with real wonder, "Do they understand the map?"

Ellen: Because we use it every single day, I think they do.
Penny: And we always compare it to the globe. What's tough about the map is it's flat. And the hardest thing about that is that China's separated onto both sides [of the map]: "Why is China there, too?"

> ... Of course, [for] some children, very little of what we are doing
> has any meaning in their lives.
>
> *Ellen:* Whether you are particularly interested in this, or whether you
> can meet the criteria ... because developmentally you're not at that
> point, yet you still must do this or you will get a failing grade.
>
> *Penny:* It's [the curriculum] very rigid in that respect.

In many areas of the curriculum, there are some expectations that Ellen
and Penny found inappropriate for many children. In mathematics, for example, telling time and place value are consistent locations of difficulty, and they
repeat the concepts over and over all year, hoping the repetition will gradually permit a dawning understanding. Penny says: "So all year long, you look
at the clock, and you pull it out when you get ten minutes, you play with the
clock and those props. You practice with them. With time, a lot of them get it,
but it's a difficult concept." Penny mentions, as well, the tension in children's
writing, between spelling correctly and invented phonetic spelling in which
children show their understanding of sound/symbol correspondence.

> The more words they can spell correctly the better. . . . But for some
> of them it [spelling correctly] just takes longer. I find it very dis-
> couraging for children who have trouble with that. Then they can't
> write anything and they don't want to write anything. It's [spelling
> correctly] important so they can be more independent, yet what's
> most important is what do they hear when they say the word, do
> they hear the sounds, what do they put down, are they close? And
> then we work away at spelling patterns.

Penny shows here her understanding of developmental patterns as children learn to write; that is, the order of learning is sound/symbol correspondence first, before grasping irregular spelling patterns (Ferreiro, 1984;
Ferreiro & Teberosky, 1982).

A further source of inappropriateness, in their perception, arises when
Ellen and Penny think of a third-grade teacher encouraging them to ask
children to make their mathematical thinking explicit in writing. The idea
that children should be able to *write* this in second grade seemed unreasonable to them, as Penny explained:

> So one of the Grade Three teachers is always saying, "Make sure by
> the end of Grade Two, if you're doing something with money,
> [when they have the answer], ask 'How do you know?'" You need
> to diagram it. They need to be able to draw a picture of how they
> solved it [or] write a statement of how they solved it.

Can they do this at that age?
I don't think they can.

They believed that many children who could talk about their answer might have great difficulty putting something on paper in a symbolic form. It troubled them that such children, whose development is quite normal (Astington, 1993), are considered less than successful—C's and D's—simply because their rate of development is different from that of the most mature children. Ellen and Penny find expectations such as those described here untenable for *all* children because they set them up to anticipate failure due merely to developmental constraints.

The Demand for Semantic Knowledge

Ellen: As I asked what excited them about what they had been doing, I was thinking to myself [that] I've got to find some way to let them get at the stuff that they're excited about, although the other part of me is saying, I don't know if I really can !!!! Because we've just got so much to do!

Penny and I both agree, there is so much there [in the curriculum] that can be quite exciting, because it *is* very rich and we work *very* hard; *very very* hard to make sure that it's fun, that it's interesting, it's appealing.

There is, for both teachers, a commitment to ensuring that these young children's learning is hands-on, with an experiential base that is meaningful and relevant to their lives. They use no worksheets and plan extensive activities that make the concepts of the curriculum meaningful and allow children to apply their skills. In social studies, for instance, an expectation is that children understand that "even though they may have been born here, that their family originated in another area and for them to investigate that area." The children did "heritage presentations," little books or posters about a specific place, talking about its culture (language, food, sports, clothes, and so forth) and showing their own relationship to the place. In one that I observed, a boy was dressed in kilt and beret and talked with aplomb about haggis and the Edinburgh castle. His booklet included photos of his great-great-great-grandfather, and this boy was clearly proud, knowledgeable, and sharing rich content on his heritage. The audience listened with attentiveness. This pedagogy for arriving at the expectation was clearly meaningful to the children, allowing them to share something of themselves and their family culture.

In the science strand on energy and water, Penny and Ellen had the children investigate objects in water (sinking and floating, repulsion and absorption, surface tension) and then design a boat. Later the children tested the boats in a creek behind the school, learning for instance that one with Styrofoam "lifeboats" all around it didn't move along the waterway but stayed put, much to the girl's consternation, and that when the wind was up, some boats could go very fast indeed. The children were fascinated by the actual results of their construction efforts, sometimes finding their predictions overturned. It is, of course, the nature of teachers' work to figure out how to create classroom events that bring an abstract expectation to life for young children. Ellen and Penny have a solid commitment to doing so by designing events rich with incident, social exchange, problem solving, planning and organizing, and collaboration among children. The result is knowledge in children that is grounded in experience.

On the other hand, the press of the curriculum documents often supports an emphasis on *semantic* knowledge rather than *experiential* knowledge. Semantic knowledge is understood at the level of language only, language being a symbol system that also represents nonlinguistic forms of knowledge. Experiential knowledge is embedded in the experiences of the body—sight, sound, scent, movement. When semantic knowledge is built on an experiential base, it makes sense for children. These different forms of knowledge are connected with different forms of memory: Schacter (1996), a respected researcher on memory, distinguishes between episodic memory structures and semantic structures in the mind. Episodic memory is grounded in the body's experience—images, sounds, scents, muscle movements, feelings, and their organization into event structures in memory. Semantic memory is based in language, language events, and organization of abstract structures.

The tension between the curriculum's thrust toward semantic knowledge and the teachers' preference for grounding in experiential knowledge manifested in situations such as the following. Ellen remarked on how important it was for the children to understand the five categories of animals, and the definitions of each, as a curriculum expectation. Simultaneously, the school—in response to parent concern—did not permit live animals in classrooms, so the understanding, for example, that amphibians have wet, slippery skin and that reptiles have dry, scaly skin could not be learned from direct experience, but only from rote memory. Rote memory of facts without basis in experience has long been recognized as the least powerful, least efficient form of learning, for it is most easily forgotten (Caine, 1997; Hannaford, 1995). For Ellen and Penny, the expectation of conceptual understanding from rote memory was simply ungrounded: they wanted experience.

The tightly prescribed curriculum content closed down other possibilities for learning and restricted these teachers' options in ways they disliked. In part it is the disjunction between a framework of knowledge as constructed by the learner in which the learner is seen as a coproducer of knowledge (e.g., Edwards, Gandini, & Forman, 1998), and the framework of knowledge in which the learner is conceived as consumer of what has already been generated by previous generations. Clearly both are necessary in schools, and Ellen and Penny, in their struggle, did not feel they had found the necessary balance.

CONFRONTING THE TENSIONS: INTEGRATION AND RELEVANCE

While it would be fair to say that Ellen and Penny have confronted the tensions in their work and acknowledge the frustrations arising from them, resolution of such struggles is a gradual and partial event in such a complex domain as teaching, especially with a new and more demanding curriculum. Yet the persistent theme in their struggle to resolve these conflicting tendencies is a double-sided focus on integration of curriculum areas coupled with ensuring meaning in the lives of children. The double-sided focus and the fact the tensions have not been resolved are clear from the following comments:

Ellen: We're told that you can manage this [curriculum], that if you over time practice this enough, you will be able to manage this. And manage means—

Penny: —you have to take what's best from it [the curriculum], what's most relevant to the children; find the best experiments—

Ellen: —lots of integration. The expectation for us as teachers is, I believe, that you integrate everything.

Carol Anne: How do you do this?

Ellen: Well, we spend hours thinking creatively about how. . . . Social Studies is a perfect example. We have this huge document for Social Studies, which includes geography and heritage, in addition to everything else, and we're supposed to cover every itty-bitty little thing and make it relevant. That's the hardest part of all, isn't it, Penny. We're not just saying, we're going to talk about "north." You can't see it, eh? So we figure if we do it [the map] every day and we show the globe every day, we have stories and poetry that relate to it, and we do the heritage books so we personalize it—

Carol Anne: So you build it up bit by bit?

Ellen: Yes, bit by bit. You take the completely irrelevant things and create a context.

Here are several illustrations of how Ellen and Penny were integrating the culminating expectations from disparate curriculum areas.

Timelines. Early in the year the children constructed personal timelines, bringing baby photographs to school and examining how they had grown and changed across the years. The culminating event was a series of installations hung across one wall, strings with clothespins holding photos and text hung in overlapping curves, the photos and writing on small cards showing a sequence from baby through to school-age stages, representing the child's life. Time became a string holding markers of change. In the teachers' description of the activity, the observer can see that many facets are drawn together. The science expectation of "an understanding of past, present, and future" is made relevant here by being connected to personal life, as is the science expectation of "identifying changes across time." Several expectations regarding writing are present, such as that cards contain complete sentences (at least one, possibly two) in describing photos or drawings, and contain "describing words." Ellen and Penny are layering multiple expectations into one complex activity.

Animals. This 5-to-6-week unit in the fall began with a hunt through old *National Geographic* magazines to cut out photos and organize them into groups, first by the children's own categories (e.g., fur and "no skin"), and later by the accepted classifications. Some groups of children applied their mathematics skills, enjoying counting how many items they had for each class of animals, with results written as follows: "73 mamels, 10 repticls, 9 fethrs [sic]," and were astonished that there could be so many mammals. As part of this unit, they spent an afternoon sketching animals in a wildlife park, watching closely and "totally entranced." They constructed three-dimensional animals from paper, tubes, boxes, and the like with corresponding habitats for their animals. Ellen commented that "there are all kinds of things covered in living systems in the [activity of building habitats that] we will be able to assess once the activity is completed."

Some of the expectations that Ellen and Penny were working with were that the children could find four "rules" by which to classify animals, and do so cooperatively in their groups. When I asked what the children learned about animals that they didn't know before, Ellen responded:

They learned that there are certain animals that are specific to North America, and that animals have particular habitats for a number of reasons, that animals need to adjust to climate changes, and available food sources. So they were learning about all this, and they were self-correcting all the time, which was letting me know an awful lot about what they had learned. They learned to think about how animals reproduce and there are a variety of ways. Many had this sense birds lay eggs; they also learned about amphibians, where some babies are born live and some by eggs.

Many misconceptions about animals, which Ellen and Penny attributed to books or cartoons, such as the Franklin the turtle series, were "unlearned." While it was difficult to ensure as much hands-on, experiential learning as they wished, representing knowledge through sketching and three-dimensional construction allowed children an experience of *making* something that encapsulated their learning in satisfying ways.

Composting. In April, elements of music, mathematics, science, and social studies were integrated in a unit on recycling and composting. The class participation in a concert during the week included a song about garbage and recycling.

> We started looking at how to take care of our environment, and they were fascinated by how much garbage there was. We started talking about garbage and composting. And in Math, in coordinate geometry, they need to understand how to read coordinates—you know, across the top, and down the side. . . . So Penny had this wonderful idea. She brought in these little planting cups that are all attached [like an egg carton]. And we labeled [coordinates] along the top and down the side and then they decided themselves what they wanted to test out for composting purposes.

The children wanted to bury carrots and fruit, meat, bones, tinfoil, paper bags, plastics, paper towels, and so forth, "and they knew that the chicken bone was buried at A5, or D11." They had 35 different items and were checking it every 2 weeks, Penny bringing it in from home where she had dug it into the ground. She said, "Some of their predictions are [really off], like they really don't think paper towel is going to decompose. And some of them really think that bone is going to be gone." They believe that using a meaningful experience to which the children have a commitment (wanting to find out what happens to their buried item) is both more developmentally appropriate and more powerful than an abstract activity on a piece of graph paper.

Although I have focused on the theme of integration of curriculum material, it is never separate, for Ellen and Penny, from the principle of relevancy—ensuring close connections to children's lives so that content has meaning—and the principle of grounding content in experiential, rather than abstract, forms. Abstract learning is difficult at most ages for all but a few students, and is particularly problematic for children under 8: they can, of course, think abstractly and hypothetically, but only in circumstances where they create freely, not where such requirements are imposed (see, for example, Donaldson, 1992; Malaguzzi & Vecchi, 1997).

THE RELATION OF CLASSROOM EVENTS, EXPECTATIONS, RUBRICS, AND REPORT CARDS

In talking to Ellen and Penny, I was interested in some very basic questions: What is on the report card, and how does it get there? How are classroom events connected to expectations? Also, I come to Ellen and Penny confused about this relationship. I have heard elsewhere that only three or four expectations per subject area are reported on in the report card, that teachers choose and describe these until the end-of-the-year report when ministry expectations are used, so that I am under the impression that the grade of A, B, C, or D is based on the three to four expectations described in the box for Language, another three or four for Mathematics, and so on. Why are teachers feeling so pressured, then, to cover curriculum and complete assessments when it won't even be reported? If only a tiny part of the curriculum shows up on the report card, why such pressure to cover the rest? It doesn't add up. Playing devil's advocate, I am wondering why teachers don't simply do the three to four expectations they choose for each area and spend the rest of their time on what they think best.

Rubrics

Ellen and Penny tell me that their main device for moving from experiential classroom events to reporting on expectations is the "rubric," and that they develop their own. Ellen says she may have about five a day, and these are not only shared with the children but may indeed be developed with them. On my April visit, the following rubric was on the wall:

What good writers do.
IDEAS—The ideas are connected and have details.
SENTENCES—Use voice in the story, like feelings and opinions.
BEGINNING, MIDDLE, and END—Story ideas are in a sequence.
          Create a good story web.
SPELLING—Spell most words correctly, words are neatly written.

Ellen and Penny's rubrics, such as the one above, tend to feel generous, address a broad range of considerations, and point to sets of things to focus on in a piece of work. Ellen and Penny's rubrics did not separate children into four levels of categorization but spoke to what everyone should attempt as solid second-grade work (that is, level 3).

Report Cards

Ellen and Penny tell me the report cards are standardized in that every child is evaluated on the same expectations for each subject area and with the same rubrics. There is no variation in what is reported on, except for a one-inch-wide box for overall comments. In this school, teachers choose and write their own expectations for during-the-year reports (rather than using end-of-year expectations from the documents), although Ellen and Penny believed that in some schools all comments were standardized. Ellen notes that because there is so little room for individual differences (with the exception of ESL or children with special needs), "the kids who don't fit that middle ground are never assessed adequately, are always going to be left out."

Also, Ellen notes that the notion of a reporting system actually being standardized is somewhat simplistic. She has two children who came from other schools and found their report cards inaccurate:

> Now one of the beauties we've been sold on about this report card
> is that everyone will be working from the same document, that they
> will all be assessed the same way, that there won't be the great
> deviations in teaching and learning that had occurred previously.
> Well! I had two students, I had to keep looking at their previous
> report cards, because I could not believe that I was reading about
> the student that I see in my room.

In one case the boy had all A's, when "this is not how I would assess him." Another child had all D's, and Ellen found him "solidly placed in the average range"; Penny added, "You just have to get past his emotional and social problems." "And so it's not a perfect system, the way [they say]. We've been sold a bill of goods," concludes Ellen.

Language-Based Grading. Ellen described some of the difficulties of moving from complex classroom life to the requirements of the new reporting system. She spoke of a child who can apply what he has learned by telling her, when he is designing a model piece of playground equipment:

Ellen: What he would do, by explaining how this would work, and
by showing me by the way he puts something together that he
has learned [for example, the expectations for Science structures
and simple machines]. He cannot write it, and he cannot read it.
I would assess him at a B: he has learned what every other
student in this class has learned, not in the same way, but he has
learned it. And he has proven to me that he knows how to use the
knowledge that he's learned. . . . But, you understand, I cannot
give him a B.

Penny: He won't be able to meet the expectations for recording in the
"Reading and Recording" aspect.

Carol Anne: So he would get a D or a C on the reading and recording,
but a B on the part he understands?

Ellen: No, because reading and recording is part of the Science curriculum. You have to be able to *record*, and that's the word that's used
in the Science curriculum.

Ellen and Penny found this emphasis on language learning in second
grade—when even Science understandings have to be filtered through
semantic knowledge and written language—disturbing in not reporting the
child's understanding.

A Massive Curriculum. Ellen noted that "we cover a huge amount that
will never be reported on." This occurs because there is not enough room
to write out what has been covered in the space of the report. Ellen and
Penny find this fact especially problematic for social studies and science
and technology, where they have a mere four lines of type to describe complex activities and expectations, as in the five strands of science. In answer
to my question about where the actual pressure to *cover* such huge amounts
of curriculum arises, if merely three to four expectations are reported on
in the report card, Ellen replies that the pressure is to provide an adequate
knowledge base for third grade and the testing at the end of it.

They call it scaffolding. So what happens, next year there will be
material that they [children] must have, those teachers are assum-
ing that there has been a base established in Grade One and Grade
Two, so that if you don't cover that, the story goes, the children are
not going to have the base.

The most salient point for Ellen and Penny is the fact that they cannot report fully on the expectations their children have accomplished

because there just isn't room. This is not surprising when the daily life over a term has to be synthesized and summarized in two pages. So it would be a mistake, in their interpretation, for anyone to think that the report card describes their program comprehensively, for it reports on a "tiny fraction" of what has been done. Here is part of our conversation on this:

Carol Anne: So you couldn't get on the report card what you wanted to evaluate?
Penny: That's right.
Ellen (exclaiming): We couldn't begin!
Penny: You're to be doing all five strands [for example, in mathematics and science] each term, and there is absolutely no way you could report on all five strands.
Carol Anne: So does the child get one letter grade in Science?
Penny: Yes.
Carol Anne: And there are two to three expectations that go into that one letter grade?
Ellen: There are a hundred!—
Penny: —All the specific expectations that you actually worked on that term!
Carol Anne: But you don't evaluate on those hundred, one of those is picked out?
Ellen: No. No, no. We evaluate them on everything we've covered. That determines the letter grade. But we only have enough space to write the words for 1/99 of it.

Here they make clear for me that they are evaluating *all* their curriculum activities, via the rubrics they construct, and out of these multiple sheets of data on the children, they arrive at a single grade. The grade, for Ellen and Penny, is an overall, holistic grade covering all they have done: the write-up beside it in the report card is a snapshot into the curriculum, describing the three or four most salient expectations.

CONSTRAINTS, CHOICES, AND POSSIBILITIES

While feeling the constraint of the standardized curriculum—its massiveness, occasional inappropriateness, and demand for semantic rather than experiential knowledge—the choice Ellen and Penny make is to try to honor both the curriculum and the early childhood pedagogies that support the learning of young children. Ellen and Penny show us three demands upon teachers attempting to honor both standardized curriculum and early childhood pedagogies. One is the challenge to synthesize massive numbers of expectations in multiple layers embedded in rich classroom events. Second, the challenge to layer expectations requires an ability to integrate disparate curriculum areas. Third, teachers must ensure that this demanding curriculum is made relevant and meaningful to young children. These challenges demand enormous creativity from teachers. When I ask Ellen and Penny how they connect expectations, rubrics, report cards, and classroom events, they say:

Penny: Just really careful integration in the planning. Being able to see how it all fits together. . . .
Carol Anne: How do you approach it? Whatever is coming up?
Ellen: I personally just get very excited. I'll wake up at four in the morning and I'll think a million things. And then on Saturday, I'll go to the Public Library, because we have nothing here [at school], and I'll search out all this stuff and I'll think, "Oh, I remember seeing something in a book, that would fit well with art here." You have to know the strand, you have to know the curriculum, all those expectations, every single one. Then, once you have all that knowledge, you can say, "Oh, I know where we could do this."

Ellen and Penny focus on integrating curriculum areas, on using rubrics as a process by which to connect classroom events and report cards, and on a holistic grading that takes into account the totality of the child's work in each subject area of the report. They are careful to design and plan classroom events that are relevant to their children, that personalize learning, and that make connections to what the children know and care about.

How are these second-grade teachers taking up the new curricula? They approach them with sincerity and attention to every expectation. Given the size of the set of curricula, what does this mean for their work? It means the struggle and tension of balancing conflicting frameworks for teaching: on the one hand, they attempt to be developmentally appropriate (by integrating curriculum and making content personally relevant), and simultaneously they are pulled onto the curriculum train of "covering" and assessing vast quantities of material. In their struggle, three tensions stand out:

1. Intense pressure and anxiety around uses of time, transitions, and frequent interruptions
2. Concern in handling expectations that they believe are untenable because they are developmentally inappropriate

3. The press to teach to semantic knowledge via rote memory, when their belief is that children's learning requires an experiential base to be meaningful and lasting

In confronting these tensions, their strategy is a double-sided focus on imaginative integration of curriculum and on ensuring that content is meaningful to children. These are considerable challenges in a climate of systemic constraints (reduced resources, time, space). Added to these challenges is the requirement of a more precisely articulated assessment, which they cope with through constructing frequent and extensive rubrics that form the basis of their evaluation: the report card grade represents a holistic mark on all that has been done, while the verbal description encapsulates three or four expectations. Throughout, Ellen and Penny show stamina, passion for teaching, and grace in their stance toward these struggles to balance conflicting frameworks, attempting to honor both children and curriculum requirements.

CHAPTER 8

Beth

Science as the Focus for Expansive Frameworks that Integrate Curriculum

This chapter shows a teacher of a combined second- and third-grade class whose passion for science provides the focal point around which she develops her program. Through three stories from Beth's classroom, we will see how she weaves together threads of curriculum and assessment into an activity-based program for these second- and third-grade children. Beth has been teaching for 12 years. She has both an undergraduate and a master's degree in Health and Physical Education, with a concentration in nutrition. While the bulk of her teaching has been in first through fourth grades, she also spent one year teaching science "on rotary" to grades one through three (which she did not like for children that age) and has taught several summer programs in science and in ESL for her school board.

In the year of our work together, there were many destabilizing factors affecting her working conditions. Beth was teaching in a school located in temporary quarters until the new building was ready in January. In the fall, the staff and children were housed in another school, the principal located in a trailer at the side of the playground. Added to the disruption of a major move in the middle of the year was increasing enrollment of new children. When I visited Beth in October, she had 24 children. By March, she had 35, and her new classroom was too small. More children were arriving at the rate of one to three per week, and the disruption of having to absorb new children was wearing on the class. Then a child in her class died unexpectedly, throwing Beth and the children into heightened emotionality and distress. In addition, they faced the stress of the third-grade standardized testing, a major weeklong assessment conducted in May.

Because of the ethnic and cultural diversity of the area, many of the children required support in learning English. Beth said 11 of the 35 children required strong ESL support and, in fact, 30 of the 35 qualified for and received some support: there was only one ESL teacher for the school. Her class also included five children with special needs, including one with Turette's syndrome, one with ADHD, and one at risk for hunger. Three children in second grade and one in third grade were below grade level: Beth offered additional language support and they went three times a week to a remedial mathematics teacher.

On the other hand, there were some ways in which Beth was offered unusual support in terms of sustaining developmentally appropriate practice for young children. Working within the theoretical tenets of the brain-based education movement (Caine & Caine, 1994; Sylwester, 1995), the principal had instituted a time schedule totally different from the production schedule organization of time usually seen in mainstream schools. Time frames were expansive, with an uninterrupted morning block of more than 2 hours, followed by a half-hour recess, then another 70-minute double period before lunch. After lunch and recess was another long block of one and a half hours. To encourage curriculum integration, teachers had weekly planning periods (during school hours) with their grade teams, and weekly meetings with the music, library, and computer teachers. The school's vision statement included mention of integrated programs, active learning, and a curriculum reflecting the needs of learners.

THE VIEW INTO BETH'S CLASSROOM: INTEGRATION OF STANDARDIZED CURRICULUM

I have chosen to highlight four aspects of Beth's teaching approach in an attempt to convey her program, and then I will describe her approach to the assessment and reporting required by the standardized curriculum. The foundation of Beth's teaching, mobilized by her love of science, is an *inquiry-based, activity-based* approach to curriculum. She builds a program on the development of children's inquiry skills through their own activity. The second fundamental of her teaching is a focus on the *integration of curriculum*, weaving many aspects together around science as the core. Third, in Beth's classroom there was a tacit structure, an undergirding, that encompassed the *creation of a caring community*. The children were permitted to act like children, "to be themselves," that is, to make spontaneous moves and to make decisions about what to do. Fourth, Beth set up what I have termed *"generous frameworks" for learning* that were expansive in their handling of time, space, and materials; her children were free to have ideas and to act upon them.

Researching Snails

When I first enter Beth's classroom I see lively children sitting in pairs on the floor in and among clusters of chairs and desks, working on the construction of elaborate mazes, playgrounds, and obstacle courses, using colored paper, Popsicle sticks, cardboard rolls, and so forth on cardboard box bases. At first I cannot see Beth at all, but rather a sea of purposeful movement, lively chatter, and the vibrant colors of cultural diversity. Pairs of children describe what they are doing to me as I move about the room, and I spot Beth working with several children in a huddle. The children are very friendly, greet and speak to me freely, and are clearly prepared for my presence among them. Later Beth tells me that most of the children were born here, but learned their family mother tongues at home. The countries of origin of the children include Sri Lanka, Pakistan, Saudi Arabia,

Ghana, Guyana, Trinidad, China, Korea, Vietnam, India, England, and France. Above the children, on each cluster of four desks, sits a "vivarium," a terrarium with earth, stones, and leaves in which four snails are living. Each child in a small group of four thus has responsibility for one of the snails, and the children insist that they can tell their snails apart.

Inquiry-Based Program. The children are creating three-dimensional constructions—their mazes, playgrounds, and racecourses—with the intent of seeing whether a question they asked about the snails can be answered. A chart of their questions on the wall reveals that they had divided all their questions about snails into two groups, questions whose answers could be found in secondary sources and questions that they could research directly. The questions vary from the type that asks, "How far can the snail move in 5 minutes?" or "Can snails do tricks?" to "How does a snail get out of its shell, if it has a door on it?" The questions reveal both the anthropomorphism of young children, who see the world in terms of the ways they understand it, and their honest attempts to grasp the nature of the snail and how it lives in the world.

The pair of children asking "Can snails do tricks?" is making a balance beam out of cardboard rolls to see if the snail can move along it. The children who asked, "How far can it go in 5 minutes?" have invented a racetrack that includes a scoreboard for each "trial" and a card on the side with many hand-drawn snails on it: a boy tells me that is the "snail audience." The visitor sees immediately the mass media cultural influences affecting the children's inspirations, their freedom to use their imaginations, and, occasionally, their incipient attempts to think about the snail in terms that move beyond ways that humans live. One pair, a girl and a boy, has made a swing and a tree, and has placed green paper on their base to suggest grass, "to make it like home" for the snail. While their representation is from a human perspective, Beth later tells me that she likes the attempt "to get into the head of the snail, in a way," to try to think about the world from the snail's perspective. Beth said, "I think they're looking out for the best interest of the snail, trying to make it comfortable, trying to make it a familiar environment." The children's questions on the wall chart reveal this mixture of anthropomorphism and attempts to understand the snail on snail terms:

Can snails eat through wood?
Do snails sleep in the water?
How do snails eat such big things?
Why do snails have shells?
Do snails stay in water when they're scared?

Beth's concern, in the meantime, was that the class finish the work with the snails in time to return them to the creek so that they could hibernate before it got too cold, or the snails would not survive the winter.

Integration of Curriculum: Layering Events with Multiple Expectations. When Beth and I chat at lunchtime about the children's work with the snails, she conveys both a broad sense of what she is attempting to do and the way that the work with snails provides a framework for integration of curriculum. She conveys a sense of layers to the goals in her classroom events, goals nested like a set of matrushka dolls.

> We're studying snails and we're trying to integrate it with language and a bit of math, art, and drama as well. First of all we did snail research, we found out all about their habitat, appearance, food, reproduction and survival methods, and then we made a snail vivarium. I look at the basic skills such as the reading, and the writing, and the scientific inquiry skills, and some basic math skills, like measuring how much water to put in: they had to measure how deep the layer would be for the soil and [for] the stones, etc. But I guess I'm also hoping that they would learn more critical thinking skills—like questioning skills. I find that to be important. Cooperative group skills [also], and I think that the most important thing is to encourage their love of learning, their sense of wonder. That's the main goal.

Beth tells me that she likes to do real research, rather than doing science out of books, because "the real stuff guarantees the children's excitement and interest." The children have done lots of writing about snails, including a "poem" in the form of a riddle that they put to music and acted out.

At various points in our discussions each session, Beth offered board documents that she uses to assist her planning, for not only is she attempting to integrate expectations across subject areas into meaningful experiences for young children, but she must also master two sets of expectations, one for second grade and one for third grade, synthesizing these into classroom events. There are so many documents that I cannot keep them straight, or their relationship to each other. If any member of the public had any doubt about teaching being complex work, they have but to look at the documents with which teachers must work to be convinced otherwise.

A Caring Community. There is a quality of warmth and open communication in this classroom that is unusual in many schools. There is, for instance, the obvious friendliness of the children toward a visitor, their curiosity about a stranger in their midst. When they gather on the carpet to meet about their snail work, it is clear that they know who I am and have been prepared for my visits. They are eager to know what they should call me, and I sense that they are intrigued by my academic title, the "Dr." (which I seldom use) but that they wish to try out. In most classrooms that I visit, the children ignore me, except for incidental exchanges, but in Beth's classroom my impression is that they want to take me into their midst, make me part of their friendly classroom community. They tell me stories about what happened at recess and ask me questions. They are interested in relating fully and richly to whomever or whatever is in the classroom.

I encounter this quality of affectionate friendliness again later in the morning when Molly, the ESL teacher, enters the room. (In this school, the ESL teacher visits children in their classrooms, in addition to various groupings of children outside the classroom.) The children greet her with evident pleasure, several crowding around her, holding her arm, intent on conversing with her. When I comment to Beth and Molly later on this affection and friendliness, Beth says, "They *are* a welcoming group. Poor Molly can hardly get away." What intrigues me is the hunch that space has been made in the program for the children's feelings and affections for others. My hunch early on was that Beth set up an expansive framework built on care of self and others in one's community that provided a foundation for the enactment of children's pro-social feelings and affections.

Generous Frameworks for Learning. The children's mazes, racetracks, playgrounds, and grassy areas for snails are constructions of settings for their research questions. The provision of a task of designing and making a setting for your research question is a broadly defined problem within which there are many possible correct moves. There are incorrect ones as well, such as forgetting the relationship between one's question and what one is constructing. The question, such as "Can snails do tricks?" (however the child as investigator defines that), sets the parameters of the research setting that he or she constructs. This is an example of a broad framework that allows children many free moves, many decisions under their own agency. There is room in such broad frameworks for children's ideas and creativity. Generating wonderful ideas is valued as the heart of intellectual activity (e.g., Duckworth, 1996). Some of the ideas the children generate are far-fetched, such as two boys who say they made "touch cars" (like bumper cars in a midway ride), and they seem to have gone a very long distance from snails. Beth handles this by asking them how they got this idea, and finishes the conversation with the comment, "Make sure you can answer your question with what you've built."

There are other frameworks evident on this day, too—a framework for generating a poem about the snail, and the frames provided by the wall charts that define fields of questioning. After my first visit, I wondered if the pattern of the day was unusual, the snails a high point in the curriculum, or whether the organization of the program as inquiry-based, integrated across several subject areas, based on a caring community, and operating within generous frameworks for time and activity was the foundation of the teaching and learning experience in this classroom.

Designing a Vehicle That Moves

In March, I go to Beth's new school, just beyond new housing and surrounded on one side by a mud field and on the other by yet more construction. The hallways of the school are wide, white, with yellow and white floor tiles polished to a high finish. There are cardboard boxes in some areas, moving in not yet complete. My visit was delayed by 5 months, first by a disruptive strike in my setting, then by the need for Beth to be sufficiently comfortable in her new setting to welcome a visitor. When I find her classroom, there are now 35 children enrolled, and more expected. I remember how difficult it is to keep a stable sense of community when the participants keep changing, yet the atmosphere of the room is similar to that of my fall visit.

Love of Science and Inquiry. What are the children doing? They are on the floor, all over the room, in small groups scattered among the clumps of desks. Each group has a rectangular thin board resting on a pile of small blocks to make a ramp. Around the ramps are straws, dowel rods, round wooden disks, little wooden frames that look like empty picture frames. On the blackboard is a chart with a column titled "Axle" and three styles of axle—a straw, a dowel rod, and a wooden barbecue skewer—and three columns labeled "Distance Travelled." I recall Beth's insistence to the children that trying out something once is never a "fair trial," they must try something three times at least for "a fair test." Each child has measured, cut, and glued set lengths of ½" wood strips into a frame about 5" x 7". They have glued four wooden clothespins, in parallel pairs, on the corners. The axle to test rests in the holes of a pair of clothespins. Pop on four wooden wheel discs and a bit of sticky tack on the end of the axle to hold on the wheels, turn it over, and presto, a little car that rolls on the floor. Let it go down the ramp to see how far it goes. Now I notice a measuring tape laid out in front of each ramp.

There are, of course, many types of problems relating to physical properties of objects to sort out as the children make their cars—such as getting the clothespins parallel so the axle is at right angles to the frame. Beth is running around trying to find thinner straws, for the fat ones won't fit well into the clothespins. During the long morning block, the cars are sent down the ramps, children checking how far they go, making adjustments to them, making notations in journals. One child calls out to me, "It goes fast!" and reports it went beyond 199 cm. As on my previous visit, there is so much going on in the room that I can catch but a fraction of it.

Beth later tells me that the children will make seats in the car and people to fit into them, and that the third-grade children will make their cars go using magnets, while the second graders will experiment with paper sails and a fan to make the car go. In working on this science curriculum material with the children, she is using documents provided by her school board, which has prepared several modules for teachers to assist the leap from ministry expectations to meaningful classroom events that permit children's understanding. Not only has her board prepared separate documents for second and third grades, it has also prepared one for teachers with a combined class of second and third graders, showing the aspects that both groups can do simultaneously and how the more mature group can be taken ahead. What surprises me is that no one else has told me about these documents: my inference is that Beth is an unusual teacher in making science the core of her program at the early elementary level. This inference is confirmed later when Beth agrees that she is more interested in science than some teachers, is often sent to workshops on science to bring back ideas for whatever school she is in, and is in fact a member of the jurisdiction team preparing science "exemplars" for all schools, documents that describe examples of science accomplishments at various stages.

After recess, the children finish up this part of the project to make a car, testing the axles, and Beth sits at a table discussing children's findings individually and looking at what they noted in their journals. Beth says to one child:

> The dowel was the best because it went the farthest?
> Did you write it down?
> Yes.
> Can you read it? (The child reads about the car going really fast.)
> I'd like you to answer this question: Which axle worked the best?

Beth's intense love of science and the way it informs her inquiry-based program is again apparent, for as the children investigated the axles, the task for the morning, they were engaged in an activity-based, meaning-centered sustained project that involved mathematics, problem solving, systematic investigation of a research question, and explorations of the relations of motion, force, and distance (all informal physics), in a relaxed, cooperative, and socially warm ambience that permitted children freedom of physical movement within a set of broad parameters for activity.

Integration of Curriculum. At recess Beth and I look around the room, and I see another example of integration of curriculum when she tells me about the "dioramas" the children are constructing in shoeboxes. She mentions that she is integrating art and literature in this activity and adds in an aside, "I don't do enough art, that's one of the areas I need to improve on." Each child is constructing in his or her diorama a favorite scene from a storybook. The one we are looking at is a scene from *Harry Potter and the Goblet of Fire* (Rowling, 2000), and Beth describes how she showed the children different techniques in working with paper, such as how to curl it, or how to cut a tree to make it stand up, and so forth. The children did a sketch first as a plan for their three-dimensional scene. I like the way the children, having built a mental representation of a scene from reading a book, are then asked to render that scene explicitly, first in a two-dimensional sketch, then in three dimensions—both tasks of real problem solving. The children are doing the dioramas slowly, over a period of time, working on them on multiple occasions. I think of how the careful construction of the scene keeps the memory of the story present all around the child as he or she works, how it invites recall of detail, of emotion, and how making a representation is a form of retelling, revisiting, a form of epistemological study to see what one knows (Cadwell, 1997; Gallas, 1994b). I also see it as a demanding but expansive framework in which to play with one's ideas about the story, furthering one's relationship to the book.

Interspersed among the dioramas on a shelf below the blackboard are folded paper cubes, pyramids, and other solid forms. Beth tells me, ". . . and I'm worrying my head off about all the other stuff we have to cover for the Grade Three test." She shows me five storybooks that she sees as connected to geometry (saying that there is lots of geometry on the test) and then points out worksheet "riddles" for geometric figures that the children created:

> I have 6 faces.
> I have 8 vertices.
> I have 12 edges.
> I am a _____.

After seeing examples of the folded-paper cubes, some children said they wanted to make jack-in-the-boxes, so Beth showed them how to make a paper-folded spring for the interior of the box. I see that Beth uses worksheets for geometry and then goes beyond them into three dimensions and into what children request. Just before lunch, I spot a boy who is finished with his research on axles making a folded paper cube: he tells me it will be a jack-in-the-box.

A Caring Community. The sense of a caring community comes across to me more strongly even than in the fall. When I arrive and get settled on a chair to observe, several children spontaneously come to greet me, remembering my name, chatting. As in the fall, there is a clear expectation that whoever is in the room will be absorbed fully into its atmosphere of affection, told stories about what is happening, and made to feel a part of the life of the room. This inclusion extends further than I would expect: after recess, the children have snacks and water whenever they wish, and just before lunch a girl offers me a graham cracker, assuring me that she has two and doesn't need both.

Beth commented that several of the newer children had difficulty working with other children in this sort of classroom. One girl had to be moved out of a group in which she was constantly out of control. Beth put her with a "boy who is very centered" and found that the strategy helped the newer girl maintain self-control. The warmth and affectionate inclusion into the community do not occur automatically thus, ensuing merely from the example that Beth sets, but require continuous thinking, problem solving, and small moves on Beth's part to sustain.

Generous Frameworks for Learning. When the children return from recess, they gather on the carpet, and Beth, seated on an old tree stump, picks up one of the books connected to geometry, Catherine Brighton's *Five Secrets in a Box* (1987). Her intention is to read them the story, discuss any problems with their cars, and send them back to work. The story, however, lasts almost 40 minutes because the children become very excited as questions about space arise and they engage in an absorbing discussion whose leaps and bounds I can scarcely follow. They raise their hands to speak, and Beth acknowledges them, letting everyone who wishes contribute. To offer the flavor of the discussion, here are several excerpts, beginning with Beth's question to the children as she holds up the book to begin reading.

> *What's your prediction about what this book will be about?*
>> You open a box and there'll be diamonds in it.
>> And reading all about Albert Einstein.
>> *This book tells about a famous scientist called Galileo. I'll write it [his name] on the board. This book is about Galileo and the telescope.*

Galileo was the first person to explore the planets. I have a book about it. The telescopes are to see things in space. [This child continues with more precise content about space, all of which I cannot catch; suddenly he is talking about quasars.

Another child offers:] You could see some planets.

Who was the first person who was born?

Adam and Eve.

[I am having difficulty following the trajectory of their thought, but Beth accepts each child's enthusiastic leap in thinking and permits the engaged discussion.]

I go to church sometimes and they say the first person was Adam and Eve and they lived in a garden.

Thank you, says Beth, that's the Christian idea of how the world started.

God is a spirit. He lives in space. They say he lives in the middle of the Universe, the spiral galaxy.

Not the Milky Way?

No, it's further [away].

What's the Milky Way?

If there's so many stars together it looks milky.

You can check on the computer and check if the world is ending.

I think God lives in the clouds.

When will the sun blow up?

In my book, it says the earth started in a big explosion.

I know where the sun comes from   a star.

You've raised lots of interesting questions, Beth laughs. There are many different ideas about how the world started. [She encapsulates the theory of evolution briefly.]

A couple more people, and then we'll read the story. [Many hands are up to contribute to this interesting conversation, with more talk about stars, bigger and smaller ones, stars draining other stars, smaller ones too close to bigger ones getting trapped, all the blazing gas that burns out the smaller one. One child concludes]:

I heard that if you go into a black hole you might go into another universe. It says in the book.

[Beth begins to read]: *My name is Virginia. I am the only daughter of Galileo. My father studies the skies at night. Me, I sleep.*

This conversation confirms for me my sense of generous frameworks for activity offered by Beth to the children. A generous framework is an expansive, elastic, or malleable use of time that includes the disposition to accept what the children have to offer as valuable. It gives space to the children's contributions within the official curriculum. The intensity of the discussion was white-hot, the children deeply engaged in conversing with one another and Beth. The comments ranged from the very knowledgeable to the echo, and the trajectories of thought leapt in many large directions, including religious belief, scientific belief, and metaphysics. The discussion was exciting to witness because of its reach, the children's enthusiasm, and the wealth of ideas offered. It was stimulating to everyone present.

Genuine conversations may be rare in classrooms, particularly if the teacher holds the children to tightly held time frames. I hypothesize that where more open schedules are tolerated in schools, a more "permeable" curriculum (Dyson, 1993) occurs in which children may insert what they bring to the education situation. Such permeability allows the children to show the meaningful connections that they are making between personal knowledge and the official curriculum: these connections provide feedback to the teacher about what to emphasize in teaching. I believe that the structure of discipline in Beth's classroom allows a broad range of free moves on the children's part, so that much more of their thinking and feeling is present in the room than in traditional classrooms. About the discussion, Beth commented: "You don't judge what they are saying. You don't want to say, oh yes, that's correct, because there are so many different religions out there. Try to be as noncommittal as possible." Given the cultural diversity of her group, it probably requires a certain moral courage to promote and sustain such lively conversation and to permit the children to engage with what they think. It is reminiscent of the provocative *discussione* of the Italian educators of Reggio Emilia (Edwards, Gandini & Forman, 1998), but there we see a homogeneous culture. It is to me even more remarkable that the value of exciting conversation can be sustained in the cultural crucible of contemporary urban schools.

Inquiry into Earthworms and Soil

When I visit the class in April, the four aspects of Beth's teaching that I have been highlighting—science as the core around which an inquiry-based program is built, integration of curriculum, construction of a caring community, and generous frameworks for activity—are vividly present and confirmed in my interpretation.

As I approach the classroom, I hear children counting by two's, getting close to 100—92, 94, 96—and suddenly Beth swings around from behind me, arms laden with yogurt tubs of worms retrieved from the fridge down the hall. Simultaneously, the children see me and run in ones and twos to greet and hug me, returning immediately to the carpet. Even the new children come, as if this is simply what is done. I continue to find it interesting that the children feel free to initiate actions in a relationship with a visitor, and that these actions should take the form of affectionate welcome, an unusual response in a public school.

Today there is an atmosphere of tremendous excitement in the room, for they are about to assemble terrariums for earthworms and begin a series of experiments on soil. On the blackboard is a plan for the morning comprising four parts:

Terrarium—Make worm habitat—4L soil, moist
Diagram
"We're all related" Art
Diorama

The children are organized in groups to measure and put soil in their terrarium, select twigs and leaves from a collection gathered on a morning walk, and send one of the group for their tub of worms. Wearing a surgical glove on one hand, they examine, talk about, and eventually place the worms in the terrarium and watch the worms. Later they draw and label a diagram of the terrarium, what they did, what they noted. When these two tasks are completed, they may continue with a complex art project with ties to their cultural heritage or work on their dioramas.

I don't think I have ever seen a group of children this excited in over 30 years in teaching. There is so much activity that I can catch only the tiniest fraction. Children move around purposefully, filling jugs with soil and pouring them into the terrarium. There are squeals as the worms are uncovered, high energy among the children, a few saying, "I'm scared to touch the worms." Some are hunched over the tubs of worms, gazing in fascinated awe, half-fear, and amazement. At one point, the noise level is so high with squeals and shrieks that Beth calms the children by asking how the worms might feel in the noise. "Scared." She reminds the class that it is a big change for the worms from the tub to their habitat, talks about moving quietly, and sends them back to their activity. I have been taking photographs for about 15 minutes, as has another adult in the room, and one group invites me to be in their photo, to me yet another sign of the inclusivity of the classroom community. By this time, many children are starting their diagrams. One boy checks with the span of his open hand the diagram on the blackboard, telling me he's checking that he got the depth of the soil right on his diagram, too.

After recess and time in the computer lab, the class returns to sit on the rug to discuss, "What did you notice about worms?" Molly, the ESL teacher, joins the class. She has laryngitis today and cannot talk. Several children

crowd around her with affection, and join her in whispering. Another child
rushes to bring a chair for her, and several others pull up chairs alongside
her at the back of the carpet, eager to welcome her, to be with her. As Beth
asks the question, the children respond, and she jots their comments on the
board as a set of reference points later for their journal writing.

> They try to get off your hand, if you touch them.
> If you wear a glove, they touch [tap] it again and again.
> They're slippery.
> *It was really nice to see how gentle you were with them.*
> They're very slimy.
> It feels like they're massaging you.
> Gooey.
> *These are all good describing words.*
> They have saddles.
> Beth and the children discuss the importance of the saddlelike
> rings on the worms, that they hold the babies, that if the saddles are
> cut the worm will die.
> *Are they hermaphrodite like snails?*
> Yes, says a child.
> [They get out a book to check the reproductive details. A child
> reads that the worm is both male and female, and lays egg sacs. A
> child is invited to the blackboard to draw an egg sac.]
> *Ben draws excellent diagrams.* [Indeed, he does. Another child
> describes how the heart muscle moves one section of the worm,
> then the next heart muscle pushes the next section of the worm.
> When the heart beats it pushes the muscles and the worm goes
> deeper into the soil.]
> I saw in the book that they have five hearts.
> *Not five hearts, but—*
> Ten!
> *Five pairs of hearts, like pairs of legs and arms.*

I hope the reader can see in the above account of the morning convincing
accounts of how Beth's love of science provides a focus around which integration of curriculum occurs. In addition, ways in which this classroom
is a caring community are interwoven in the ongoing experience of everyone in the room. The expansiveness of the time frames is encompassed in
the morning plan, and in the generous time given to hearing the children's
observations about the worms. As usual, the children's comments are both
more perceptive and more creative than any curriculum planner could
anticipate.

BETH'S STANCE TOWARD THE STANDARDIZED CURRICULUM: INTEGRATION AND COMPLEXITY

Because Beth showed me more board documents, and articulated their fit with standardized expectations from the ministry, and because Beth participated in the science group constructing exemplars for other boards and schools, I had the impression that she is both a master teacher of science and also a teacher less frustrated by the standardized curriculum than some less experienced teachers. When I asked if her teaching had changed with the imposition of the standardized curriculum, she said she did not see the new expectations as the focus of changes to her teaching. She felt that she was "getting better at integrating" curriculum, using science as the focus and creating meaningful, interesting classroom events as the foundation for the development of complex understandings about the world. She told me her teaching didn't "feel any different," that "I'm doing the same thing I did before but I feel kind of—like a stress, trying to get through it all." My interpretation is that Beth felt increased stress resulting both from the size of the curriculum and from increasing, unstable class size, but also felt an authority to use discernment in selecting a focus and omitting trivial outcomes.

Discernment in Teaching and Assessment

Just as Beth offered the children expansive frameworks of time and activity in which to plan, initiate, try out, and evaluate their actions, and just as she set up an underlying classroom organization that permitted spontaneous free moves for the children, she permitted herself a stance of discerning judgment in working with the standardized curriculum. Her experience while teaching fourth-grade math had taught her that it was impossible to honor the curriculum while approaching it in a linear way, expectation by expectation. She had found—as has everyone I have talked to, both formally and informally—that the massiveness of the standardized curriculum alone makes it undoable in a linear, fragmented pedagogy. Thus she had returned to a more holistic approach that focused on the integration of curriculum, and felt free to make her own best judgments about its emphases. Beth emphasized "enduring understandings" (big concepts) and big dispositions toward living in the world, such as the development in children of inquiry skills, of close observation (of snails, earthworms, soil, axles), of critical thinking and self-assessment, of social cooperation with partners.

As an example of her detailed work with inquiry skills, she commented in an aside once, "Myself, I need to work on questioning skills." In many teachers, and certainly beginning teachers, such a comment would refer to the teacher's range of techniques for asking questions of children. That, however, was not what Beth meant. Her notion of working on questioning skills was attuned to children's learning.

> My plan is—I'm going to start it in the next week or two—where they come up with different questions. First they have different experiments that they do [on soil] and then they respond to them in their science journals. And they come up with questions at the end of each of those [experiments]. At the end, they look at all their questions, and any more that they might have, and then they choose one question and design their own experiment. Then they do it.
> *So you really see if they've understood the inquiry process.*
> Then you look at what's a good question.

This emphasis on generating good questions is an example of discernment in teaching. It is a judgment about the overall capacities that it is important to foster in young children in order to contribute adequately to their education. I think back to Beth's comment in October: "The most important thing is to encourage their love of learning, their sense of wonder, that's the main goal." Beth, in promoting children's ability to generate questions, is teaching children how to be generators of knowledge rather than mere consumers of knowledge made by others before them. She offers these children of diversity tools that assist the development of capacities that will contribute to their ability to take up professional roles within society.

The Relation of Teaching Events, Expectations, and Report Cards

Because of the complex classroom events that defined Beth's teaching approach, I found myself asking her repeatedly to help me understand how she moved from these elaborate contexts for learning (school life lived in three dimensions rather than in the two-dimensionality of paper-and-pencil tasks) to a grade on the report card of a standardized curriculum. How did she move from a curriculum characterized by integration to a report card separated into subject areas? How did she arrive at grades of A, B, C, and D when working so much in three dimensions? I have three accounts of her descriptions of this process, and each time she showed me different support documents from her school board. I will attempt to summarize this elaborate process so that its complexity is graspable, but the reader should be cautioned that only an outline of what Beth does can be communicated in this limited space.

First, Beth layers multiple expectations from several areas of the curriculum—language, art, science, and math, for instance—into rich and supportive contexts for learning. I am calling these contexts for learning "classroom events" to distinguish them from the simpler "lessons" and "lesson plans" of traditional teaching, in which a one-to-one correspondence is assumed between what the teacher teaches and what the student learns. Lessons are straightforward and presume a unidirectional relationship, that of curriculum content passed to child. Rich classroom events are multidirectional and permit relationality in many directions, such as child to child, teacher to child, child to teacher, and child to curriculum, in addition to curriculum content passed to child. The difference is like the difference between a mind on a leash, willed to a single goal, and a mind in a field free to roam within a set of boundaries. These classroom events are rich and expansive and encompass big ideas, like how specific animals make their way in the world, why Galileo studied the stars, how to make a machine that moves, or how to learn to function as a contributing member of a group. The small stuff (learning to diagram and graph, to edit one's writing, to punctuate) is learned within the context of a larger vision, so one can see the technical used in the service of something to which it contributes.

What does Beth use to evaluate the children's work?

> I use everything I can. Anecdotal notes, pictures [photographs], the students' actual work, looking at what they've done, how much help I've given them, all their little tasks as we went, and the final performance task, did they actually work with their partner, . . . writing up the results, and then they share them with the class.

Beth's account suggests a rich, expansive, balanced approach to assessment, taking into account many aspects of functioning and many modes of demonstrating competence. These modes include oral talk, written accounts, and actual performance in addition to both formative processes (all the little tasks as children proceed) and summative evaluations (children's report of findings or the final performance task).

How does she do all of this? First, she feels free to focus on the big concepts of greatest importance to her—the inquiry skills, the notion of fair testing, of cooperative work, of sharing findings in a variety of forms. By using "enduring understandings" (Wiggins & McTighe, 1998) as a curriculum magnet around which to gather up the filings of tiny menial outcomes, she is able both to integrate program and to reduce the mental fragmentation of trying to deal with long lists of specific small expectations. But I am still wondering what processes Beth uses to arrive at that wretched little grade for a subject on a report card, that reduction and encapsulation of so much lived life and learning to a single alphabetic unit that is expected to represent all the variegated capacities, skills, accomplishments, and vulnerabilities of a child. The grade of A, B, C, or D is a crude metaphor for all that is going on in a child's head, heart, and hands, the crudest of metaphors for learning. How does a teacher who works in far more sophisticated, complex, and subtle ways arrive at such grades?

Beth shows me a list from one of her board documents that outlines seven recommended forms of assessment, none of which is a worksheet to grade, and tells me the ones she uses most. She uses her own observations and anecdotal notes (such as, "Did they come up with a question, a prediction; did they do the fair test, then record the results and share them?"). She works with the children's journals and what they are able to record in drawing and writing. She constructs checklists for herself of four levels of response to the activities using board documents for descriptors and scales. She constructs rubrics in "kid language" from these checklists, simplifying them so children can do a self-assessment (for instance, a "fair test" rubric), and she uses a rubric or set of criteria for the final performance task. She talks about working "backwards by design," a common phrase in this school board, of thinking through a big final task (making the car, publishing a book, designing an experiment) and offering children support in developing the techniques, tools, and capacities necessary to accomplish the big task. She kept a booklet for each child with their previous report card in it, and "blank pages to record significant information (health concerns, daily observations, conferences with parents and other teachers, miscue analysis, etc.)." She also kept a file folder "portfolio" for each child: along with their work, it included child assessments of the "smarts" (multiple intelligences, see Gardner, 1999) they thought they used to complete work, what they learned, and what they would do to improve or change it.

Her approach to assessment thus is holistic and discerning. It is holistic because it takes into account everyday aspects of children's lives in supportive contexts for learning. It uses implicit teacher judgments in addition to external markers of success, and it takes broad processes—"everything"—into account, not simply a list of selected expectations, nor simply pieces of paper used as an "evidentiary warrant" (the phrase is Sharon Murphy's, personal conversation, 2000, York University) for learning. Her approach is discerning because she takes the authority to select the most important big features of the curriculum that she wishes to address. Beth commented on how the science coordinator encouraged teachers to do one module really well and to go slowly. For instance, the "making cars" module encompassed many rich processes of design and inquiry and might last five months. This is in contrast to teachers who feel compelled to rush through five strands of science. Beth told me she selects from the board documents the material that will be her focus:

> Like I left out some parts and picked out others that I wanted to focus, that were more relevant.
>
> *So you feel free to take what you wish from this document. You don't take it as something you have to use exactly as it says?*
>
> No. And actually, they recommend that you don't. They recommend that you adapt, pick and choose, throw it out, change it.

Beth's stance toward the board documents is that they are offered as guidelines, as possible routes to bridging the distance between classroom events and the abstract ministry expectations. Beth commented that the board documents, with specific ideas for what to do in classrooms, "really hand it to you on a platter," and were, she thought, especially helpful for beginning teachers. One other teacher in her school was trying out some small parts of the making cars module.

How does a teacher sustain a stance of discernment in the face of the list-laden ministry documents that outline her legal obligation in teaching? I have mentioned Beth's participation in constructing science exemplars for the Ministry of Education for the region, and also her membership in the board science group working on aspects of science teaching. As noted earlier, when I asked her how her teaching had changed since the standardized curriculum, she felt that apart from a previous failed attempt to teach math in linear ways, it had not changed very much, although she was more stressed about "covering" curriculum content. She referred to the work of Derek Hodson (Hodson & Hodson, 1998) on scaffolding, and his argument that teachers should offer their own thoughts—adult thinking—to "give them guidance." Beth was more conscious of inserting her thinking now, whereas previously she had been more concerned that she might "stifle their creativity and their thinking." She made a change in her teaching in response to a new understanding from the academic community, rather than in response to the standardized curriculum.

I asked Beth whether she thought that the ministry expectations, exhaustive as they attempted to be, included all the important learning in the classroom. No, she said, and continued with four ways in which they did not reflect children's learning. These four ways included lack of recognition of higher-level thinking skills in language learning, lack of recognition of children's motivation and effort, the problem of fragmented subjects, and the lack of recognition of the importance of children's interests in contributing to learning. She mentions the general view that the language document was poorly conceived and written, in part because "the ministry had to bring it out really quickly." She complained that its focus is grammar and "little facets of writing." She finds her board's documents on writing and reading far more comprehensive and elaborated and works with them. Beth finds the mismatch between the necessity of integrating curriculum to handle massive amounts of content and the requirement of grading subjects separately an awkward disjunction: "They've compartmentalized all the subjects, but you have to take all that and try to integrate it all." The role of children's interests in motivating and pushing learning is also not recognized in the standardized curriculum: "I'm trying to focus on what we call enduring learnings, and then look at what the children are interested in, how they're going to bring in their questions. They're writing poems about worms and bringing stuff from home. I'd rather follow their interests."

In commenting on what she saw omitted from the standardized curriculum, Beth did not mention the co-construction with her children of a caring classroom community. I infer that this fundamental aspect of Beth's teaching practice may be tacit, one of the hidden things she does that is difficult to make explicit to others. It is a taken-for-granted aspect of her practice to show the children repeatedly and in detail how to treat each other, how to be gentle with the worms, how to welcome a visitor, to be aware the worms don't get too hot if your tables are near the windows, to think in repeated small ways of how to care for those around you. It is her stance toward the world: she is herself gentle and kind, never raising her voice, using underlying frameworks for learning (expansive structures of inquiry-based, integrated curriculum) to provide the structure of discipline in the room. The children were free to make spontaneous decisions about how to care for others within the general structures—when to offer a cracker to a visitor, when to help a friend whose paper-roll balance beam wouldn't stick to its base. Much of the joy in the room arose from spontaneous gestures of reciprocity, mutual exchange with others.

CONSTRAINTS, CHOICES, AND POSSIBILITIES

The four aspects of Beth's teaching that I have highlighted here—inquiry-based pedagogy; integrated curriculum; expansive frameworks for handling time, space, and materials; and an inclusive, caring community—resulted in developmentally appropriate practice for her second-and-third-grade class. What permits Beth to sustain such pedagogy in spite of the imposition of the standardized curriculum? What range of choices does Beth imagine for herself as a teacher? Beth, I argue, had a sense of free moves as a teacher, just as she offered the children a broad range of free moves in her classroom. She had, perhaps, a stronger sense of authority in making discerning decisions about curriculum than many teachers. From where did she get such authority? First, her frequent work on board documents and on ministry exemplars gives her the knowledge that her teaching is an example to others. Second, the support of resource consultants years ago in teaching her how to structure an integrated curriculum gave her confidence: she had the practical knowledge to integrate curriculum successfully and consistently across both subject matter and time. Third, her principal's institution of a school schedule with expansive frameworks for handling time may well be the single most important factor in supporting Beth's pedagogical decisions, for she was not working against the grain in her school. If we ask what led Beth to make this set of pedagogical choices, we can see it is a combination of belief, values that prefer an intellectual (i.e., inquiry-based or questioning) approach and a strong sense of community, a sense of authority about her teaching (though her gentleness and humility might render this invisible), and supportive structures for uses of time and colleagiality at the institutional level.

Unquestionably, the learning going on in Beth's classroom was outstanding in the richness of the material offered, the stimulating ideas generated by the children in response to meaningful activities, and the quality of their responses both intellectually and as members of a caring community. In addition, the principal informed me the following year that Beth's students, predominantly an ESL group, had indeed scored very well on the third-grade standardized testing. High test scores without teaching to the test were one result of her approach: other results included a caring community, highly developed capacities for thinking and inquiry, love of learning, and radiantly happy children.

CHAPTER 9

The Mechanistic Versus the Holistic

The Hope for Early Childhood Education in Prescriptive Settings

It helps to see these portraits of eight teachers in light of broader social processes at work in education and in society. Mainstream traditional approaches in education have always been contested (Dewey, 1997/1938; Edwards, Gandini, & Forman, 1998; Montessori, 1964), and there is no singular agreement about how learning should occur for young children, no matter what is imposed at policy levels. In this chapter I will set the research findings in a larger theoretical context, then outline four approaches to the standardized curriculum of the teachers in this study and the consequences of these approaches. Next I will speculate on what moves these teachers toward these approaches, and consider implications for efforts to support early childhood education in schools. The chapter concludes with an Epilogue that brings the reader up to date with the teachers several years later.

THE PARADIGMS OF CLOCKWORK MECHANISM AND HOLISM

The language of a culture tacitly carries a deep metaphor within it, like an underground stream (Bateson, 1979; Bowers & Flinders, 1990). The metaphors that cultures live by are encoded in their language and shape what we "see" as "reality." Western thought accommodates at least two major conflicting metaphors or worldviews. These two conflicting metaphors are the view of the world as a machine and the view of the world as a living organism. The metaphor of the world as a machine argues that if we can but figure out how things are put together, then the world will be predictable and controllable. This is the modernist view of Western science, based on Newtonian physics and clockwork mechanism. If the world is viewed as predictable and controllable, then a linear set of instructions, followed step by step, should produce what it is we want. A list of instructions is a prescribed or prescriptive way of doing something meant to guarantee a quality product or assembly. Doing things in prescribed ways results in prescriptive technologies that are mechanistic because the worldview is of a machine to be assembled.

Prescriptive technologies define the range of responses that humans can make in a specific context. Prescriptive technologies were increasingly applied to all areas of living in the West during the 20th century, from the 4-hour feeding schedules for infants of the 1940s and 1950s, to the development of the fast food industry. In the latter part of the 20th century, prescriptive technologies were applied to social institutions such as hospitals and schools for purposes of meeting standards of efficiency and accountability. Prescriptive technologies are frequently referred to as the factory model or the machine model, or are described as mechanistic, rationalized, or outcomes-based (Apple, 1979; Bowers & Flinders, 1990; Giroux, Penna, & Pinar, 1981; Spady, 1994).

This mechanistic worldview is no longer considered adequate in science, as new theories of chaos, complexity, and various holistic systems theories work with phenomena that the Newtonian world omitted (Bohm, 1980; Davis & Sumara, 1997; Gleick, 1987). Called into serious question by postmodern views, these new theories of science show evidence of a world that is unstable (rather than in equilibrium); dynamic (rather than finished in design); and interrelated in all aspects, with implosions into the new (e.g., viruses such as SARS) when events interact. The new science views the world as unpredictable at individual levels, and the consequences of actions, in the multiplicity of their effects, as uncontrollable. These new sciences have had a demonstrable impact on business, medicine, and many institutions in society (Doll, 1993; Ferguson, 1980; Senge, 1990).

Holistic theories have entered education as well as these other areas of society. The metaphor that sees the world as a living organism argues that the world is holistic, interconnected in entirety, that it is complex, responsive, relational, dynamic, fluid, and unfinished. Priority is given to relationality and to understanding relationality in the world, to functioning as an organic community, to stewardship of others and of the world (e.g., Edwards, Gandini, & Forman, 1998). Holistic technologies are based on a systems theory view of the world in which causation is believed to be multiple, complex, interconnected, unpredictable, and ultimately uncontrollable. The world is viewed not as a stable, finite order to be deduced correctly, but as responsive, unplanned, unpredictable sets of competing, interlocking subsystems with multivaried effects on each other, which further effect what happens (Bateson, 1979; Dahlberg, Moss, & Pence, 1999; Doll, 1993; Gleick, 1987). If the world is complex, interconnected, and integrated, then all parts live in response to other parts, jointly cocreating interactive effects that further shape other effects. Doing things in relational, reciprocal, collaborative, emergent ways results in holistic technologies because the worldview is of a living organism to be sustained. The most complex practice of the early childhood education field is an example of sets of holistic processes (as in Edwards, Gandini, & Forman, 1998; Jones & Nimmo, 1994).

Education, nonetheless, still operates in mainstream jurisdictions as if the machine metaphor holds true. Because the conflict between mechanistic and holistic worldviews is deeply embedded in our culture at all levels of functioning, teachers are also embedded in this conflict, experiencing the struggle of being pushed and pulled in shifting directions in our thinking. Teachers reflect different aspects of these two contradictory worldviews as they respond to both paradigms as they appear in the details of daily life. The problems and challenges of teachers are systemic, not individual, and each portrait here shows one unique response made by a particular individual to the complexity of contemporary teaching.

FOUR APPROACHES TOWARD THE
STANDARDIZED CURRICULUM

Among the eight teachers, I found four approaches toward the standardized curriculum. One approach was a linear, lockstep approach, segmented by subject. A second approach was to ignore the standardized curriculum and resist its coercion toward practices that the teacher considered inappropriate for young children. The third was to hold a linear and an integrated approach in tension. The fourth approach attempted to integrate curriculum across subject areas into rich, expansive, meaningful classroom events. I will discuss each of these approaches, their consequences, and implications for the teachers and their children.

The Linear, Lockstep Approach

Two of the teachers, Ann and Susan, both teaching first-grade, had taken up the standardized curriculum using a linear, lockstep, segmented-by-subject approach as their dominant teaching practice. By *linear,* I mean a tendency to focus on one or a few expectations at a time and then move to another expectation. By *lockstep,* I mean a tendency to contain content in designated time frames. By *segmented-by-subject,* I mean a tendency to break the school day into time frames that each contained a specific segment of the curriculum—language, mathematics, science and technology, social studies, the arts—and to teach these separately from each other. Characteristics and consequences of the linear, lockstep segmented approach in this research were (1) brief time frames each containing technical tasks for a particular subject; (2) a focus on the agenda of the technical task; (3) piecework assessment of the technical task, now taught and presumably learned; and (4) an inability to return to the task for reteaching or reassessment if it was not learned by some children.

Brief Time Frames. Brief time frames ranged from 10 to 30 minutes in length. Brief time frames meant that teachers and children were switching mental focus frequently and learned not to sustain activity beyond a brief period. It is interesting that the length of these brief time frames is similar to segments on television and the switch in mental focus provided

by ads. I argue, following Jackson's revelations about the hidden curriculum in schools (1990), that what such frequent switches in focus teach children is that normal life is spent doing small technical tasks that change every
few minutes. Certainly, such work is a feature of many manufacturing and
prescriptive technologies for production in adult life, the fast food industry providing a vivid example. Business corporations in particular might
argue that teaching children to take for granted as normal a fragmented
experience of time and work, with multiple quick shifts, is extremely useful, since this is a prevalent feature of the contemporary adult work world.
Yet many corporations have broken from this model of work organization
and developed group collectives with control of a project (such as some
car manufacturers and the communications and technology industry) with
much success (Senge, 1990).

Recent studies of frequent switches in mental focus and of multitasking
suggest that these ways of functioning are debilitating to humans and drain
energy (Norretranders, 1998; Sallot, 2001). Susan, who utilized taut time
frames the most intensely of all the teachers, was, as she described, physically exhausted and mentally drained at the end of each school year. The
effects of stress on human health are well documented elsewhere; suffice
it to say that such situations are unhealthy for teachers, and the long-term
impact on children has not, to my knowledge, been researched. My own
judgment was that uses of time in brief teaching-to-task bites was unhealthy
for all concerned. The children could do it, but the children were also relatively wary and subdued. My hypothesis is that affective responses (especially positive ones) are flattened under tautly held time frames used for
technical tasks, and that this repression of affect erupts in unpredictable
ways, for instance in forms of resistance to curriculum, or in forms of worry
and depression turned inward against the self.

It is not simply the use of the brief time frame that is so stressful and
debilitating, but the fact that the activity emphasizes technical tasks that
are evaluated externally. Each change of task means a new demand for
performance, and without a chance to relax, to breathe out between time
frames, the body is left always in hyperalert modes of functioning. The issue
is whether this use of time is too stressful for young children and their teachers. Just as 4-hour feeding schedules for infants in the 1950s were unresponsive to individual babies, so such brief time frames for technical tasks
by subject are unresponsive to children's rates of development and pace
of learning and the natural rhythms of child activity. Jones and Reynolds
(1992) note that children's learning requires a breathing-in phase and a
breathing-out phase, just as breath itself has two phases. A breathing-in
phase is similar to taking in new information and working to demand with
it. Breathing out is a relaxation phase, a chance to play and have the activ-

ity of the body under one's own control. I argue that brief time frames used for technical tasks are inappropriate and unhealthy for young children and may have the unfortunate impact of destroying children's concentration span for sustained activity. The development of concentration and an ability to focus on sustained activity is a requirement for any serious efforts of design, research, problem solving, creative production, or tackling big world problems.

Focus on the Technical. As we saw in the chapters portraying Ann and Susan, there was present in their teaching a technical focus in each time frame. Ann, for instance, attempted to teach an English structure for comparisons to ESL children, or the notation of one-half in fractions. Susan attempted to teach skip-counting patterns while using a calculator, speed in doing addition problems, and technical aspects of writing while children wrote about a group set of perceptions of their walk. When the technical is emphasized as the focus, then what might emerge from the children—their own background knowledge, their ideas, thoughts, hopes, and intentions—is invariably overridden. The children's personalities as thinking, feeling human beings are overridden by technical concerns. But the technical is not, in itself, very interesting: it becomes valuable in the service of making something else. It isn't that it is not important: technical facility is crucial to the accomplishment of excellence in any field. But when technical aspects are made the focus, then larger goals in whose service they are held are diminished. This particular standardized curriculum, in which each item gets one space on the list, thus equates the trivial with the highly significant, as if there were no difference. Teachers, when they take up the curriculum in a linear, segmented way, thus are led to give the trivial objective as much emphasis as more substantive goals. The curriculum itself appears to provide this directive, if teachers attend to it expectation by expectation.

Both Susan and Ann complained (as did Ellen and Penny) that teaching isn't as much fun as it used to be. "It's not fun for us and it's not as much fun for the kids" (Ann). "We feel as though we've taken a lot of the fun out of learning" (Susan). I submit that it is their new emphasis on the technical aspects of each subject that has in large measure reduced their capacity to keep learning embedded in enjoyment and pleasure. Prescriptive technologies that focus on technical precision remove enjoyment because they leave no room for human invention, for joyful reciprocity and responsiveness to each other and the world. In that regard, they are inhuman. Ellen's apology for the children's work to craft arctic settings in plasticene because it was not on the curriculum is instructive here: because it was not in the service of some technical focus for mastery, she could hardly justify it, though it allowed the children to express in creative ways their understanding of arctic life, and their representations immediately showed the limits of their knowledge and where a teacher might move to build on that. A standardized curriculum conceived in terms that emphasize the technical thus creates the strange reality that teachers *apologize* for creating lively contexts for learning, because the content of children's interests is not mentioned in the curriculum.

Piecework Assessment. Because the government report cards require grading by subject, and because the curriculum expectations are described in linear lists with a technical emphasis, and because of the massiveness of the curriculum, these teachers who take up the curriculum in a linear, segmented-by-subject approach believe they must evaluate every expectation for every child with a justification for the grade provided by an evidentiary warrant (work samples, worksheets, or other concrete documentation). It is the interaction of curriculum massiveness, technical skills as a focus, and the requirement of grading by individual expectation with evidentiary warrant that results in piecework assessment. As both Ann and Susan pointed out, the curriculum is so massive that once an expectation was covered and assessed, they could not go back and redo it for those children who might have missed it, for other expectations not yet covered demanded attention and assessment. The curriculum taken up in a linear, segmented approach creates a never-resolved pressure on teachers to move ever more quickly. As previously mentioned, each brief time frame is like the boxcar of a freight train, encompassing some specific container of goods (e.g., Susan testing children's use of the calculator to skip-count), and once the time frame has moved by, that boxcar on the curriculum train is gone. The more massive the curriculum, the longer the curriculum train, and the faster the teacher must go to make it fit into the finite time of the school year. As the linear curriculum train passes by, some children "get" some boxcars (a B grade) and miss others (a D) because they "went by" at the wrong time for them. Susan said she was spending an additional week on a.m. and p.m. because it was so difficult for the children. Ironically, the government's wish for more rigorous curriculum and more accountability in assessment leads occasionally to tremendous inefficiency, as hours are spent attempting to teach something children cannot easily learn. I know of no research base that demonstrates that such abstract and technical understanding is helpful to the intellectual development of a 6-year-old.

Incapacity to Return to Expectations Already Taught. The most problematic assumption in the linear, segmented approach is the assumption that what has been covered or taught in a piecemeal fashion has therefore been learned. This assumption of a one-to-one relation between teaching and learning is a foolhardy illusion well understood by most teachers, who see remarkable and far-fetched interpretations by children of what seemed straightforward. Teachers recognize this foolhardiness when they complain, as Ann did, that the children are not developmentally ready for this curriculum. The inflexibility of the linear, segmented approach, in leaving teachers unable to return to difficult concepts the children don't yet grasp, is one example of how prescriptive technologies that specify exactly what is done remove reciprocity by their very design, for teachers are left unable to be responsive to the actual facts of children's learning.

In the linear, segmented approach, if the curriculum is to be taught, then the teacher must move on. Susan described how she could not go back, asking me if I understood the point, and Ann commented on this aspect as well. With a linear approach, the essential feature is that the curriculum train keeps moving. Such an approach overrides completely any individual differences in developmental pace and maturity, and any differences in cultural background outside the frame of school learning.

The worrisome implication is the possibility that *less* learning occurs in linear approaches. First, less learning is probable if unlearned expectations cannot be redone, since new ones must be taught. This leaves children with the knowledge that they do not understand what was taught. We do not know the long-term consequences of knowing one does not know, but loss of intellectual confidence is presumed (Katz & Chard, 2000). Second, less learning may occur because positive social processes and affect are flattened, depressed, or deflected by a focus on the technical and by the curriculum train. I speculate that the main learning could be merely how to sustain the pace of the curriculum, rather than deep foundational knowledge of the major symbol systems of society.

Resistance: Ignoring the Standardized Curriculum

In my casting for teachers for this project, I was fortunate to net one teacher who decided to leave teaching. I say fortunate because teachers who have left the school system are plentiful statistically but unavailable once they have departed. Janet's resistance to the standardized curriculum was that of an intellectual with a well-developed critique of its limitations. She saw the focus on technical skills as superficial and overly limiting and the structure of the curriculum as narrow and rigid. In her comments to me about the rapid changes in teaching there was a tacit sense of moral outrage that what was being asked of very young children was simply wrong, and possibly harmful. What was wrong was the "pushed-down" academic content that she deemed inappropriate for 6-year-olds, the focus on superficial technical skills like capitals and periods rather than on understanding. But she was especially outraged that she was required to classify such young children by grades of A, B, C, or D and found the template for reporting on children's progress inadequate because much of what occurred in her classroom could not be reported on. It could not be reported on because, in her view, only three expectations were included per subject. In sum, Janet was appalled by the standardized curriculum and its format, which suggested a linear, lockstep, segmented-by-subject approach. She could not teach using the linear approach suggested by the format of the documents because it contravened every fiber of her teaching identity.

From my observations of Janet's classroom, I believed that much of what occurred fit the curriculum documents for first grade, but that it could not be documented in the linear, segmented way suggested by the shopping-list format of the documents, nor was it accessible to the sort of classification into four levels of grades that the reporting system now required. The stance that Janet communicated to me was that in her school, she had no choice about how to proceed, and no room to maneuver in deciding how she might adapt to this reporting system.

The forms of Janet's resistance to the standardized curriculum were both passive and consciously active. Her basic mode of surviving during the year of our research was to retreat into her classroom and withdraw from colleagues: "Basically, I close my door." But her sense of isolation from colleagues and principal was exacerbated by her sense of alienation, that she was the only teacher in the school who did not use worksheets, and her sense of integrity and surprise at her colleagues' compliance with a linear approach: "People are abandoning what they know and believe." Her profound sense of isolation and alienation from the culture of teaching, in which she had earlier been a favored member, also led to conscious acts of resistance, such as quietly sabotaging the grading system by giving "humane" grades, and refusing to include a pamphlet with report cards that she felt was "propaganda." Also, she actively encouraged others not to include the pamphlet. Such acts are risky in a system requiring compliance from teachers, and surrounding teachers with networks of legal obligation from both provincial policy levels and from teacher unions. Her context became unworkable for her, and she left teaching.

Linear and Integrated Approaches in Tension

Corrine in kindergarten, and Ellen and Penny in second grade, were moving in the direction of integrating curriculum while still feeling the sharp tug of using linear time slots. The principal quality of a tension is the experience of being pulled in two contrasting directions simultaneously.

These teachers struggled with both directions, and both approaches were present throughout their teaching. What was remarkable to me was that Corrine had absorbed so much knowledge of early childhood education as a field while on the job. Corrine and Ellen both had fewer than 5 years teaching experience and were still thus in the early stages of developing their teaching practice. I saw, in their classrooms, qualities characteristic of both linear and integrated approaches, as outlined in this chapter in the section on a linear, segmented approach and on an integrated approach to curriculum, and I won't repeat them here.

Could I see anything specific in their situation to justify calling theirs a third approach? What I say here is speculation, based on my impressions of the emotional and psychic dimensions of teaching and learning. The children seemed happier and more relaxed than where the dominant approach was linear: they were, to me, less wary and subdued—they felt free to share their tummy and backaches, for instance. The quality of their work also seemed richer and more complex than in linear classrooms. However, the teachers seemed as stressed as those using more linear approaches, perhaps more so, because they continuously absorbed the uncertainty of being pulled simultaneously in two contradictory directions about how to teach. They showed more reflection and more striving after something in their talk with me, whereas those with a more linear approach gave me the sense of a treadmill beyond which they could not see or move. Those torn between approaches were ever-restless, anxious, but also more hopeful than those more set in linear approaches.

Integration of Curriculum as a Stance

Three teachers, Grace, Beth, and Janet, had well-developed holistic pedagogies prior to the standardized curriculum, and approached the standardized curriculum as a context in which to continue to coconstruct with children expansive and richly engaging classroom events that shared power with children, drew on their interests and desires, and kept school a life lived not solely on paper but also in the three-dimensionality of meaningful social and material experiences. The teachers crafted their pedagogies to permit children to make decisions themselves about what to do, permitted children to plan, to initiate activity, to think, to be social. Their notion of integrated curriculum was expansive in that multiple expectations across several subject areas were occurring simultaneously. In fact, the sense of lived life was so strong that one knows a single teacher could not evaluate all these potential expectations for each and every child in a quid pro quo way or she would never be able to teach or get the activities going. These teachers selected via a process of discernment what was most significant for attentiveness and judgment, and experienced professional teachers excel at the discerning judgment that keeps a classroom thriving. Because Janet removed herself first from considering the standardized curriculum a part of her pedagogy and then from teaching itself, I prefer to continue this section referring to the two teachers who did fully consider the standardized curriculum.

There were seven characteristics and consequences (they are hard to separate) that I found in classrooms that integrated curriculum. I am framing these characteristics in terms of direct effects of teaching practice on emotional tone, qualities of energy, and the sense of dynamic relationality in classrooms. These characteristics were expansive time frames, social processes occurring alongside curriculum content, a climate of psychological safety, a sense of community, a quality of intellectuality (not merely academics), teaching as the supporting of complex contexts for learning (not merely instruction), and openness to emergent processes.

Expansive Time Frames. Both Beth and Grace used broad expanses of time into which many ways of being were incorporated. These expansive time frames permitted children many freely chosen moves of planning and decision making, of generating their own ideas, within an overall supportive framework provided by the teachers. It was as if the children lived in a field of possibilities bounded by a broad set of parameters, rather than being held on a tight leash that kept them pointed at a single small objective. There were many "objectives" all present simultaneously, ready to be navigated depending on what was meaningful to the children.

Social Processes Alongside Curriculum Content. In both classrooms, children's spontaneous social engagement with each other occurred organically as an aspect alongside specific curriculum content. Broad social processes, shaped by the value of working cooperatively together, and under the control of both children and teacher, provided a rich context of sociality in which curriculum content was embedded. These classrooms supported the importance of talk—children's talk with each other—as a domain in which much learning occurs. I believe talk was valued by these teachers as central to making curriculum meaningful for children.

Psychological Safety. In these classrooms where curriculum was integrated and children's spontaneous actions were permitted, and where in addition the teacher actively promoted the children's care for each other in addition to hers for them, there was a palpable sense of ease, of relaxed alertness among the children. They were bright-eyed and deeply engaged in interesting things to do and think about. They felt safe sharing their ideas with each other and with a visitor. The fact that they felt safe permitted high levels of curiosity and engagement with content, so that higher levels of discussion, questioning, and care for others emerged. These classrooms felt joyful.

Sense of Community. Grace and Beth created something beyond psychological safety, a sense of community larger than any single individual within it. They created a sense of something larger to which each member of the class belonged and contributed. The social processes in their classrooms were at a level of group care and stewardship that any political jurisdiction might envy. They were preparing children not simply for mastery of a standardized curriculum but for a citizenship in which one thinks carefully about others and attempts to act in supportive ways for humans and for ecologies of the world.

Intellectuality. Grace and Beth's classrooms included many rich and meaningful discussions about important processes to young children, from birthdays and the lives of insects to galaxies, stars, and concepts of God. In these communities there was a quality of acceptance, a feeling that one did not have to watch what one said but that all ideas and thoughts could be turned over and investigated for what they offered and for their limitations. Discussions were rich and thoughtful and deeply meaningful, and both communities conveyed a stance that big ideas mattered. This quality of intellectual dimension was not unique to Grace and Beth's classroom, and certainly some of the other classrooms displayed similar moments.

Complex Contexts for Learning. Traditional teaching is thought of as instruction. In classrooms where curriculum was integrated, teaching was not merely a matter of direct instruction. Instruction was clearly present in continual processes, but was embedded in complex contexts for learning. In other words, what was offered to children was a much richer classroom than mere instruction provides. The children were offered social and material worlds of experience, and any direct instruction was attached to meaningful experiences.

Openness to Emergent Processes. Beth and Grace both liked to use the outdoors, to go for walks and investigate beyond the confines of the school itself. In their classes there was a disposition to make room for emergent processes, such as Grace inviting a child fascinated by a snail on a sidewalk to bring it into class for the day, or Beth permitting children to express their interesting ideas about space and about God before reading the story she had chosen. Wide-ranging discussions that included controversial statements were permitted, and the children were allowed to explore them. These teachers were interested in what children noticed, in their thoughts and feelings and what they revealed about themselves. This quality of openness to others and to experiences was, in fact, a quality present in all the classrooms of teachers who shared an early childhood education background.

Those teachers who brought more holistic philosophies to teaching also brought a discerning judgment about what expectations to emphasize. They felt free to dismiss some expectations as trivial, unlikely, unmemorable, or inappropriate for their children and to omit them. But more significantly, they had developed a sense of judgment about what expectations they would emphasize. Both Grace and Beth consistently worked with big goals, such as crafting caring communities and understanding living things. Beth was preparing to work on children's questioning skills and their capacity to ask interesting questions. Although I saw in all teachers a tendency to nest expectations in multiples, gathering up a handful at a time, teachers with linear approaches nested three or four expectations within a subject area, whereas teachers with holistic pedagogies nested many expectations and nested those across subject areas. Their thinking was broader and encompassed more. Their assessment processes were also more holistic, taking every aspect of the children's functioning they could think of into account as evidence, whereas those with linear approaches tended to focus more closely on the three targeted expectations for a subject area that were to appear on the report card.

In sum, then, strategies of teachers with holistic pedagogies and a focus on integration of curriculum included:

1. A stance of selective discernment toward expectations, emphasizing some and omitting or dwelling less on others
2. A nesting of expectations into multiples across subject areas as they integrated curriculum, rather than nesting by subject area
3. Broad, complex frameworks for classroom events as rich experiences that required expansive time frames
4. Use of board documents that supported integration and the development of enduring understandings

WHAT MOVES TEACHERS TOWARD
THE MECHANISTIC OR THE HOLISTIC?

Teachers are human beings, and as such take up standardized curriculum in nonstandardized ways. They take it up in ways that are complex and highly diverse and reflect their uniqueness and individuality. Why are some teachers able to integrate standardized curriculum into developmentally appropriate practice, and others drop DAP and move toward linear, segmented, prescriptive pedagogies? My attempts below to uncover from my data what leads teachers in either direction are offered with the hope of provoking further discussion. I see four influences that lead toward the mechanistic and three that lead toward holistic values that sustain DAP.

Mechanistic Influences

Linear Documents. I believe that the documents themselves are the single most compelling dimension coercing teachers toward a linear, segmented treatment of classroom life. Because they have the authority of law, their very structure as a prescriptive list of what "will" be done is a compelling force in the lives of teachers. While the documents do not, in themselves, say *how* the curriculum is to be learned, the structure of their format implicitly suggests a linear approach. Because the documents take the form of lists, by subject area, of hundreds of expectations for learning and performing, they look like a neverending shopping list. When shopping, we select one item after another from a shelf or bin, and put the items in a cart to take home. When teachers speak of "delivering" this curriculum, it is as if each item (expectation), once taught, is considered to be safely deposited in the cart of the child's brain. This is a highly mechanical view of learning.

Time as a Production Schedule and the Curriculum Train. Most aspects of Western life treat time as a production schedule, and schools have always functioned with timetables by subject. As massiveness of curriculum increases, time frames become smaller as more material to be learned is pressed into smaller time fragments. And if an expectation remains unlearned after the time segment has passed (such as clock time), then it remains unlearned because something else has to be taught in the next time slot. The curriculum train moves on, in a production schedule use of time, whether the child is on it or not.

Grading Young Children. I would have to say that this particular standardized curriculum and its reporting practices has the power to change the *thinking* of teachers of young children from consideration of children's development in mastering the basic symbol systems of the culture to thinking about differentiating children into four categories and defending that separation according to crude rubrics that take little of the complexities of learning into account. Janet thought this tendency occurred because of the demand that learning be observable and measurable.

What policy levels may not recognize is that a "measurement" of learning, in the form of a grade, is a *metaphor* for learning. Measurement of knowledge, because it is metaphorical, is not the same thing as the knowledge itself—just as a map is but a portion of the territory it describes (Bateson, 1979). Yet the metaphor (the grade) is given the status of a fact because there was an external measure: this is a fallacy of logic in mainstream education startling in its inadequacy.

Grades of A, B, C, and D are unfitting metaphors for young children's learning. I argue, in fact, that teachers of early childhood years (K–Grade 2) *not* be required to grade children in this manner, for such grading is presumptuous, forced, contrived, and unreasonable. Adequate time and space in which to learn are necessary as a condition prior to judgment of learning. A linear, segmented curriculum in particular shows no knowledge of the rhythms of living of young children. Malaguzzi (1998) said it beautifully:

> One has to respect the time of maturation; of development; of the tools of doing and understanding; of the full, slow, extravagant, lucid, and ever-changing emergence of children's capacities; it is a measure of cultural and biological wisdom. (p. 80)

To judge young children prematurely is surely not only unwise but morally unconscionable as a society.

School Culture That Promotes Prescriptive Technologies. In this study, the tone of a school was set by the principal. In Ann's and Susan's school and in Janet's, the focus was "delivering" the standardized curriculum in a production schedule in which assessment and evaluation were focused on grading for report cards. The school culture could be described as traditional or prescriptive or mechanistic. In these schools, the principal had no interest in what I was doing with their teachers (though they had given permission for their teachers to participate), and I hypothesize that their lack of interest occurred because what I was doing was outside the bounds of traditional curriculum and its prescriptive evaluation.

Holistic Influences

Were there factors that seemed to point teachers in the direction of more holistic practice and the possibility of sustaining DAP? I suggest three factors: these concerned school culture that promoted more holistic values, and professional development through contact with professional literature or colleagues.

School Culture That Promotes Holistic Values. Grace and Corrine taught in schools where their principals each had some early childhood education background. These teachers did not have to defend the ways their teaching was developmentally appropriate. Ellen and Penny taught in a school where the principal promoted an arts focus, and this offered openings for broader thinking. Beth taught in a school where the principal promoted brain-based education and integration of curriculum. Where the principal promoted a more holistic vision—whether early childhood or not—a stance of sustaining DAP was more welcome and possible.

Professional Development through Academic and Board Literature. Several teachers—Corrine, Beth—spoke of their board's emphasis on enduring understandings, and used this focus as a rationale for not becoming lost in the maze of hundreds of expectations. Beth's teaching had been influenced by science writers, and Grace spoke about the impact on her teaching of the educators of Reggio Emilia. Ann was taking a course in ESL. For these teachers, continuing engagement with literature of interest to them was a possible factor in supporting their faith in holistic values.

Professional Development through Collegial Support. The teachers who were sustaining DAP through holistic values all had at least one supportive professional colleague with whom to share their work. Corrine's teaching developed toward the developmentally appropriate because of the impact of an exemplary early childhood colleague who drew her into a professional development early childhood group. Grace saw her principal as particularly supportive of her approach. Ellen and Penny had each other. Janet, in isolation in a prescriptive milieu, could not bear to stay in teaching. I think it difficult to overestimate the importance of like-minded colleagues in sustaining early childhood practice in schools. Whether peers, principal, or teacher mentor, the role of colleagues in the field in sustaining others is a necessary inspiration.

Speculative Hypothesis. Beyond these points I can but speculate, and readers will have their own theories. We might say that strong ECE background helped in sustaining DAP and holistic teaching practice, but among the six teachers interested in integrating curriculum was one with no ECE background, but rather much experience in science. Perhaps solid ECE background is one form of experience leading to constructivist, developmentally appropriate teaching, and there are any number of other routes by which to arrive at pedagogies of integration. A year after the research, Ann, in her view, felt she had drifted away from developmentally appropriate practice without realizing it. An intriguing question for teachers to ask themselves is how much their teaching has changed without conscious realization or reflection on their part. Is the belief that practice is developmentally appropriate sufficient to sustain a teacher, even when her dominant pedagogy is linear and mechanistic? In both this study and my earlier one (Wien, 1995), one teacher thought she was developmentally appropriate when her dominant practice was prescriptive. Why did Susan move away from activity centers to a production schedule organization of learning yet retain those centers virtually unused? Did having them in the space offer the illusion of appropriate pedagogy?

Let me try a theory. I speculate that unless teachers have had some powerful intervention beyond traditional B.Ed. background (such as ECE, a professional development group, or a powerful mentor or colleague), it will be too difficult to override the power of the combination of

1. Linear, segmented curriculum documents
2. Time designed as a production schedule
3. Required grading for report cards
4. A prescriptive, mechanistic school culture

Where linear expectations and production schedule uses of time occur together, I speculate that teachers without more specialized background cannot see beyond them to any other possibilities. Because the curriculum documents have the force of a set of rules, teachers may well lose sight of the distinction between curriculum content and pedagogy. With no powerful experience of alternatives, it becomes impossible to imagine any other way to use time but the linear production schedule in a one-to-one match with curriculum. This is what I would suggest at this time, but it is a provisional set of factors that I am prepared to see differently.

IMPLICATIONS

What are the implications of this research for policymakers and administrators, for teacher professional development, and for teacher preparation programs? I hope that policymakers and administrators (principals and superintendents) can see four things. First, to support a stance of selective discernment in teaching, teachers require *a sense of free moves for themselves*—the right to design, with some choice, the events in their classrooms. The use of prescriptive processes in education is misplaced because humans, who include intention, ethics, and creative joy in their ways of being, cannot be reduced to machines carrying out someone else's prescriptions for teaching. Second, in order to be able to synthesize multiple expectations in complex classroom events, *teachers require support from school boards and other educators.* Teachers who are able to integrate standardized curriculum are potent resources, and their colleagues need their help. Documents, videos, and online and consulting resources could also be helpful in this regard. Third, in order to integrate curriculum, *teachers require expansive time frames with few interruptions.* Breaking the vise of production-schedule uses of time is perhaps the most helpful practice an administrator can offer to open up the range of possibilities for teachers (e.g., Caine, 1997; Wien & Kirby-Smith, 1998). Finally, one of the nastier implications policymakers should watch is the unintended consequence that more educated and thoughtful teachers leave teaching when it becomes too prescriptive: it is a terrible irony that the most educated teacher, Janet, felt compelled to leave teaching.

Teacher professional development programs declined in our area with the imposition of massive funding cutbacks in education, yet they are to me the single most important thing a teacher can do to sustain her teaching in developmentally appropriate ways. The results of this study convinced me to begin an in-service program that supports early childhood pedagogies, a program launched in 2003 within my Faculty of Education. But such programs have to be voluntary and allow a choice of commitment, rather than impose more prescriptive requirements that teachers must do.

Collegial support is simply a basic requirement for teachers of young children. Grace and Beth both mentioned the role of resource consultants in supporting their understanding of how to integrate, Corrine changed grade in order to work with a colleague, and Janet left teaching because she was so isolated. Teachers might appear to teach alone, but in reality require colleagues with whom to plan, reflect, and restore psychic energy.

Implications for preservice teacher education are more delicate. One does not wish to discourage teachers before they start. It seems important, nonethess, that the consequences of the linear, segmented approach be confronted, and other possibilities for organizing curriculum be experienced in preparatory programs themselves, if teachers are to have a chance to sustain early childhood education in schools.

EPILOGUE

In March 2002, the teachers and I gathered for an afternoon colloquium to discuss the draft manuscript. Each had read the whole and saw themselves in relation to the other teachers. What had happened to them in the 18 to 30 months since the research, and how had their teaching changed?

Grace continues to teach kindergarten but after losing her principal has changed schools, always pursuing the most supportive principal she can find for her pedagogy. She has been increasingly influenced by the Reggio Emilia approach rather than curriculum documents: this has affected her design of environments and her emphasis on relations with parents. In 2003 she said, "It's getting harder," and moved yet again. As the book goes to press, she has again found a supportive principal and a school where she is very happy.

Corrine moved from kindergarten to first grade in order to have a colleague with whom to work. She had many of the same children for a second year, and found a benefit to be her previously established rapport with parents. She felt more relaxed about the curriculum, able to retain "big time frames," and simultaneously felt that she had to vigorously defend every integrated, developmentally appropriate way of engaging curriculum to her partner, who was traditional but open-minded.

Penny has moved from teaching second grade in a team with Ellen to teaching third grade. She says she's much more relaxed about covering curriculum, in spite of the weeklong standardized assessment in May. She says she's getting better at integrating curriculum, that her teaching has not changed, but her stance toward it has: "I've lightened up a bit on the curriculum and reporting . . . it's a game sometimes." She doesn't find evaluation "the be-all and end-all" or worry even if she has "to fudge things a little bit" on the report card.

Ellen is teaching fourth grade and says her teaching has changed in that she uses the arts in a bigger way, "particularly drama; it really feels very play-based when you're using drama." She uses drama as a focus for integration of curriculum and invites children to improvise with her in roles from stories, integrating the stories with science and social studies. "The thing that strikes me most about the curriculum is the imbalance in power, that's been my goal in drama—allowing them to take the lead and have the power."

Beth is teaching kindergarten in another city and school board. She was initially quite nervous about working with younger children, thinking her observation skills needed honing, but was relaxed about the curriculum. She finds herself amazed by the children, "what they think and say," continues an integrated pedagogy, and comments on how much she learns from the children.

Ann is teaching second grade. She was startled in reading the manuscript because she saw herself turning into a teacher she did not want to be. "I don't like myself," she said after reading the full manuscript, "I don't want to be the kind of teacher I see here, I don't like what I'm turning into." She had thought her teaching was developmentally appropriate until she read portraits of other teachers and saw her teaching in relation to them. For Ann the colloquium was a time of concern, of lament for her teaching, and of feeling goaded to rethink her pedagogy.

Susan declined to attend the colloquium, citing overwhelming work pressures in addition to a household move. She expressed relief—"It's just one thing less"—when I reminded her that research participation is always voluntary, that of course she didn't have to come—it was an invitation. She is still teaching first grade and feels "more in control of" her teaching: "I don't think I'll be as burned out" in June.

Perhaps the most interesting situation is Janet's. After two years in business, she said she knows she is "a teacher at heart, I want to teach." She came back to schools with the intention of working with children with special needs, those children "who were slipping between the cracks." In her own classroom, without the pressure of the pace of the standardized curriculum, she felt she could teach with integrity in developmentally appropriate ways and do something for children who would be lost in regular classrooms.

My overall conclusion is that it is more difficult for teachers to offer developmentally appropriate practice in elementary teaching than it was before the imposition of the standardized curriculum, but that it is not impossible for teachers who know how to integrate curriculum and who have a sense of authority and discernment about what is important and what is trivial in lists of expectations. A passion around which to focus teaching (science, drama, Reggio Emilia) seems to energize teachers. It is also clear that integrating curriculum is more intellectually challenging than a linear, segmented approach, and the latter is "less fun" and both mentally exhausting and physically draining for teachers.

I come away from this research project amazed at what teachers are able to make happen for children in their care, amazed at their tenacity and love—both of their work and of children—and saddened that my culture has been so hard on them in recent years, and my government so determined to impose prescriptive controls. My argument here has been that such moves are misplaced for very young children, whose entry into society should surely include vivacity, wonder, and the joy of being alive. I thank the teachers for sharing their teaching lives with me, their struggles, their craft as they design complex events in classrooms. And I marvel at their capacity to liberate learning from the confines of linear documents, to connect it to deep meaning, intention, and attachment in children and so bring forth the world to them.

Brief Description
of Methodology

Part of the challenge of research and writing is crafting a design that is doable within the confines of other requirements for one's work. The school board had given approval for the research project in May 1999. In the school year 1999–2000 I worked with five teachers and in 2000–2001 a further three. I wanted at least two exemplars from each early childhood grade—kindergarten, first grade, and second grade. How did I find them? I approached teachers who graduated from the undergraduate program in which I teach, graduate students in the field, or members of a professional development group, all within the same board. In two cases, names of teachers were suggested by a resource consultant. No one whom I approached declined to participate. In some cases, I believe this was a combination of a trusting relationship previously established and, where I was unknown to a teacher, a sense that the topic mattered. While teachers may join the work with ease, as the researcher ultimately responsible for what gets written, I know the tightrope that I walk between balanced reports and crafting portrayals that participants agree are accurate, fair, and authentic. I will not attempt to publish a portrayal without the cycle of work that includes participants' input and agreement, but I also would not publish an account that I did not think was adequately complex or one that ignored challenges the teacher encountered.

I visited each teacher in her classroom two or three times (again, determined by the parameters of the doable negotiated against depth of data). Each visit consisted of an observation in her classroom of 2 to 3 hours and an audiotaped interview of 45 to 70 minutes. During the observation, I performed a running record, attempting to record in as much detail as possible what was occurring in the classroom. I attempted to word-process these field notes, fleshing them out and including my inferences (so marked) where I thought necessary, within 2 weeks. These were mailed back to the teachers in case some detail might be useful in their teaching and also to indicate to teachers the limitations of the outsider's view. The outsider understands but a fraction of the whole understood by the teacher, and requires the teacher's agreement that what has been conveyed is sufficiently reasonable and telling in relation to the important events in the classroom.

During each interview, I asked the teacher what was going on during the observation time that was significant to her. Her response both revealed her agenda and provided a check on my observations. The interviews proceeded as a discussion about the day's teaching and learning intermixed with my questions about the standardized curriculum, assessment, and reporting in relation to the events of the day. The reason I insist on observing in my research, in addition to interviewing teachers, is that such observation grounds teacher talk. Values, beliefs, feelings, and reactions to their own work are all embedded in the detail of the daily events we have shared. It also furthers my understanding to share that context, and it provides much richer data when it comes time to write.

The interview tapes were transcribed verbatim, either by me or, during 2000–2001, by my graduate assistant, Sara Furnival. Either way, the process of listening again to the teacher's voice, transcribing, or checking and correcting the transcription calls up further thoughts, themes, issues, and engagement with that teacher's particular situation. Listening to tapes scaffolds the next step.

Generally a visit generated 6 to 12 single-spaced pages of field notes and 20 to 30 pages (double-spaced) of interview transcript, so that each portrayal was based on 70 to 100 pages of data. After the visits, I wrote a first draft of a portrayal for each of the teachers, describing her teaching practice and how she was working with the standardized curriculum, assessment, and reporting. These drafts, about 25 pages in length, were given back to the teacher for her comments, alterations, and feedback. I made revisions in accord with their feedback, fixing grammar and negotiating with them if they wanted omitted something I preferred to include. What kinds of revisions did they suggest? Sometimes it was alterations to their own words, quoted from interviews, when they were dissatisfied with how they said something. Sometimes they asked me to remove comments that they felt were critical of other teachers or their principal: these were removed. When teachers were comfortable with the revised portrayal, I asked permission to share the portrayal more widely.

Once the portrayals were fully developed, setting them side by side can lead to further interpretation, both for readers and researcher. In March 2002, the participants met together for a one-day colloquium after each had read a draft of the full manuscript. This discussion and the teachers' present whereabouts are included in the Epilogue in Chapter 9.

Discussion Questions

1. While Grace and Janet appear on the surface to have similar ECE beliefs, values, and pedagogies, their responses to the standardized curriculum are very different. How might we account for that, beyond different temperaments?
2. Both Ann and Janet think it is the reporting system that is driving the changes toward less developmentally appropriate teaching, through the demand for observable, measurable evidence categorized into four levels for grading. Ann couldn't see how her teaching had changed until she read the manuscript. What else helps teachers see their teaching in broader contexts? How can teachers respond if they see themselves teaching in opposition to their beliefs and values?
3. What might we imagine leads Susan to use such tight, narrow time frames? Why are taut time frames seen as the solution to too many expectations to teach? Why does she keep the early childhood centers that she scarcely uses or observes?
4. What are the implications of "fudging a little bit" in report cards? And what does that mean? What are the differences between ethical requirements in teaching and requirements for accountability?
5. Which teachers seem able to coax the highest-quality work from the children? Which classrooms produce work with the most depth and breadth of thinking, complexity, sophisticated use of basic skills, and value to the children? Are there any inconsistencies?
6. Given the data for these eight teachers, what systemic supports are necessary for teachers to sustain developmentally appropriate practice in schools and liberate their teaching?

References

Allen, R. (2001). Cultivating kindergarten: The reach for academic heights raises challenges. *Curriculum Update* [newsletter]. Association for Supervision and Curriculum Development.

Apple, M. (1979). *Curriculum and ideology.* London: Routledge & Kegan Paul.

Astington, J. W. (1993). *The child's discovery of the mind.* [Developing Child Series], Bruner, J., Cole, M., & Karmilof, A. (Eds.). Cambridge, MA: Harvard University Press.

Bateson, G. (1979). *Mind and nature: A necessary unity.* New York: Dutton.

Bohm, D. (1980). *Wholeness and the implicate order.* London: Ark Paperbacks.

Bowers, C. A., & Flinders, D. F. (1990). *Responsive teaching: An ecological approach to classroom patterns of language, culture, and thought.* New York: Teachers College Press.

Bredekamp, S. (1987). *Developmentally appropriate practice.* Washington, DC: National Association for the Education of Young Children.

Bredekamp, S., & Copple, C. (Eds.). (1997). *Developmentally appropriate practice* (revised edition). Washington, DC: National Association for the Education of Young Children.

Bredekamp, S., & Rosegrant, T. (Eds.). (1992). *Reaching potentials: Appropriate curriculum and assessment for young children. Vol. 1.* Washington, DC: National Association for the Education of Young Children.

Bredekamp, S., & Rosegrant, T. (Eds.). (1995). *Reaching potentials: Transforming early childhood curriculum and assessment. Vol. 2.* Washington, DC: National Association for the Education of Young Children.

Brighton, C. (1987). *Five secrets in a box.* Markham, Ontario, Canada: Fitzhenry & Whiteside.

British website: *www.dfes.gov.uk,* retrieved January 14, 2004.

Burts, D., Hart, G., Charlesworth, R., & Kirk, L. (1990). A comparison of frequencies of stress behaviors observed in kindergarten children in classrooms with developmentally appropriate practices versus developmentally inappropriate instructional practices. *Early Childhood Research Quarterly, 5*(3), 407–420.

Cadwell, L. B. (1997). *Bringing Reggio Emilia home: An innovative approach to early childhood education.* New York: Teachers College Press.

Cadwell, L. B. (2003). *Bringing learning to life: The Reggio approach to early childhood education.* New York: Teachers College Press.

Caine, R. N. (1997). Maximizing learning: A conversation with Renate Nummela Caine. *Educational Leadership*, 54(6), 11–15, March.

Caine, R. N., & Caine, G. (1994). *Making connections: Teaching and the human brain*. Menlo Park, CA: Addison–Wesley.

Caine, R. N., & Caine, G. (1997). *Education on the edge of possibility*. Alexandria, VA: Association for Curriculum Supervision Development.

Carter, M., & Curtis, D. (1999). *Thinking big: Extending emergent curriculum processes* [Videotape]. Seattle, WA: Harvest Resources.

Cohen, D., Stern, V., & Balaban, N. (1997). *Observing and recording the behavior of young children*. New York: Teachers College Press.

Crain, W. (1994). *Theories of development: Concepts and applications* (4th ed.). Englewood Cliffs, NJ: Prentice-Hall.

Curtis, D., & Carter, M. (2003). *Designs for living and learning: Transforming early childhood environments*. St Paul, MN: Redleaf Press.

Dahlberg, G., Moss, P., & Pence, A. (1999). *Beyond quality in early childhood education and care: Postmodern perspectives*. London: Falmer Press.

Damasio, A. (1994). *Descartes's error: Emotion, reason, and the human brain*. New York: Putnam.

Davis, B., & Sumara, D. (1997). Cognition, complexity, and teacher education. *Harvard Educational Review*, 67(1), 105–125.

Davoli, M., & Ferri, G. (2000). *Reggio tutta: A guide to the city by the children*. Reggio Emilia, Italy: Reggio Children.

Dewey, J. (1997). *Education and experience*. New York: Simon & Schuster. (Original work published 1938)

Doll, W. (1993). *A postmodern perspective on curriculum*. New York: Teachers College Press.

Donaldson, M. (1992). *Human minds: An exploration*. New York: Penguin/Allen Lane.

Duckworth, E. (1996). *"The having of wonderful ideas": And other essays on teaching and learning*. New York: Teachers College Press.

Dyson, A. H. (1988). *Multiple worlds of child writers: Friends learning to write*. New York: Teachers College Press.

Dyson, A. H. (1993). *Social worlds of children learning to write in an urban school*. New York: Teachers College Press.

Edwards, C., Gandini, L., & Forman, G. (Eds.). (1998). *The hundred languages of children: The Reggio Emilia approach—Advanced reflections* (2nd ed.). Greenwich, CT: Ablex.

Elkind, D. (1990). Academic pressures—too much, too soon: The demise of play. In E. Klugman & S. Smilansky (Eds.), *Children's play and learning: Perspectives and policy implications* (pp. 3–17). New York: Teachers College Press.

Ferguson, M. (1980). *The Aquarian conspiracy: Personal and social transformation in the 1980's*. Los Angeles: Tarcher.

Ferreiro, E. (1984). The underlying logic of literacy development. In H. Goelman, A. Oberg, & F. Smith (Eds.), *Awakening to literacy* (pp. 154–173). Portsmouth, NH: Heinemann.

Ferreiro, E., & Teberosky, A. (1982). *Literacy before schooling*. Exeter, NH: Heinnemann.

Filippini, T. (1997). The school as a system. Lecture, North American Study Tour to Reggio Emilia, Italy.

Franklin, U. (1999). *The real world of technology* (Rev. Ed.). Toronto, Ontario, Canada: Anansi.

Fraser, S. (2000). *Authentic childhood: Experiencing Reggio Emilia in the classroom.* Scarborough, Ontario, Canada: Nelson.

Gallas, K. (1994a). *The languages of learning: How children talk, write, dance, draw, and sing their understanding of the world.* New York: Teachers College Press.

Gallas, K. (1994b). Art as epistemology. In K. Gallas, *The languages of learning: How children talk, write, dance, draw, and sing their understanding of the world* (pp. 130–146). New York: Teachers College Press.

Gardner, H. (1999). *Intelligence reframed: Multiple intelligences for the 21st century.* New York: Basic.

Genishi, C. (Ed.). (1992). *Ways of assessing children and curriculum: Stories of early childhood practice.* New York: Teachers College Press.

Giroux, H., Penna, A., & Pinar, W. (Eds.). (1981). *Curriculum and instruction.* Berkeley, CA: McCutchan.

Gleick, J. (1987). *Chaos: Making a new science.* New York: Penguin.

Hannaford, C. (1995). *Smart moves: Why learning is not all in your head.* Arlington, VA: Great Ocean Publishers.

Hendrick, J. (Ed.). (1997). *First steps toward teaching the Reggio way.* Upper Saddle River, NJ: Prentice-Hall.

Hendrick, J., & Chandler, K. (1996). *The whole child: Canadian* (6th ed.). Scarborough, Ontario, Canada: Prentice-Hall.

Heshusius, L., & Ballard, K. (1996). *From positivism to interpretivism and beyond: Tales of transformation in educational and social research—The mind–body connection.* New York: Teachers College Press.

Hoban, L. (1985). *Arthur's loose tooth.* New York: Harper & Row.

Hodson, D., & Hodson, J. (1998). From constructivism to social constructivism: A Vygotskian perspective on teaching and learning sciences. *School Science Review, 79*(289), 33–41.

Hohmann, M., Banet, B., & Weikart, D. (1978). *Young children in action.* Ypsilanti, MI: High/Scope Press.

Jackson, P. (1990). *Life in classrooms.* New York: Teachers College Press. (Original work published 1968)

Jones, E., Evans, K., & Rencken, K. (2001). *The lively kindergarten: Emergent curriculum in action.* Washington, DC: National Association for the Education of Young Children.

Jones, E., & Nimmo, J. (1994). *Emergent curriculum.* Washington, DC: National Association for the Education of Young Children.

Jones, E., & Reynolds, G. (1992). *The play's the thing: Teachers' roles in children's play.* New York: Teachers College Press.

Kamii, C., & DeVries, R. (1993). *Physical knowledge in preschool education.* New York: Teachers College Press. (Original work published 1978)

Katz, L., & Chard, S. (2000). *Engaging children's minds: The project approach* (2nd ed.). Scarborough, Ontario, Canada: Prentice-Hall.

Kirby, S., & McKenna, K. (1989). *Experience, research, social change: Methods from the margins.* Toronto, Ontario, Canada: Garamond.

Kohn, A. (2001). Fighting the tests: Turning frustration into action. *Young Children, 56*(2), 19–24.

Law, B., & Eckes, M. (2000). *The more-than-just-surviving handbook: ESL for every classroom teacher.* Winnipeg, Manitoba, Canada: Peguis.

Lawrence-Lightfoot, S., & Hoffman-Davis, J. (1997). *The art and science of portraiture.* San Francisco: Jossey-Bass.

Lewington, J., & Orpwood, G. (1993). *Overdue assignment: Taking responsibility for Canada's schools.* Toronto, Ontario, Canada: John Wiley & Sons.

Malaguzzi, L. (Ed.). (1996). *The hundred languages of children* (catalogue to the exhibit). Reggio Emilia, Italy: Reggio Children.

Malaguzzi, L. (1998). History, ideas, and basic philosophy: An interview with Lella Gandini. In C. Edwards, L. Gandini, & G. Forman (Eds.), *The hundred languages of children: The Reggio Emilia approach—advanced reflections* (pp. 49–97). Greenwich, CT: Ablex.

Malaguzzi, L., & Vecchi, V. (1997). *Shoe and meter.* Reggio Emilia, Italy: Reggio Children.

Masson, H. (1940). *Hockey* [painting]. Art Image 2 compiled by Monique Briere. Montreal, Quebec, Canada: Les Editions l'Image de l'Art Inc.

McBratney, S. (1994). *Guess how much I love you.* Cambridge, MA: Candlewick Press.

McCain, M., & Mustard, F. (1999). *The early years study: Reversing the real brain drain.* Toronto, Ontario, Canada: Ontario Children's Secretariat.

McRel (n.d.). Content knowledge—History of the standards. From www. Mcrel.org/standards-benchmarks/docs/purpose.asp. Retrieved January 14, 2004.

Miles, M., & Huberman, M. (1984). *Qualitative data analysis: A sourcebook of new methods.* Beverly Hills, CA: Sage.

Ministry of Education and Training. (1997). *The Ontario Curriculum: Grades 1–8.* Toronto, Ontario, Canada: Government of Ontario.

Ministry of Education and Training. (1998). *The kindergarten program.* Toronto, Ontario, Canada: Government of Ontario.

Ministry of Education and Training. (2000). *Exemplars: Writing.* Toronto, Ontario, Canada: Government of Ontario.

Montessori, M. (1964). *The Montessori method.* New York: Schocken. (Original work published 1912)

Norretranders, T. (1998). *The user illusion: Cutting consciousness down to size* (Jonathon Sydenham, Trans.). New York: Penguin.

Piaget, J. (1962). *Play, dreams and imitation in childhood* (C. Gattegno & F. M. Hodgson, Trans.). London: Routledge and Kegan Paul. (Original work published 1951)

Piaget, J. (1971). *The construction of reality in the child* (M. Cook, Trans.). New York: Bantam. (Original work published 1954)

Portelli, J., & Solomon, P. (Eds.). (2001). *The erosion of democracy in education.* Calgary, Alberta, Canada: Detselig.

Read, K., & Patterson, J. (1980). *Nursery school and kindergarten: Human relations and learning* (7th ed.). New York: Holt, Rinehart & Winston. (First edition published 1950)

Rowling, J. K. (2000). *Harry Potter and the goblet of fire.* Bloomsbury, British Columbia, Canada: Raincoast Books.

Royal Commission on Aboriginal Peoples. (1996). *Final Report.* Ottawa, Ontario: Government of Canada.

Sallot, J. (2001). Please turn off your radio before you read this. *Globe and Mail* [Toronto], Monday, August 6, p. 1.

Santrock, J. (1996). *Child development* (7th ed.). Dubuque, IA: Brown & Benchmark.

Schacter, D. (1996). *Searching for memory: The brain, the mind, and the past.* New York: Basic Books.

Senge, P. (1990). *The fifth discipline: The art and practice of the learning organization.* New York: Doubleday.

Sheridan, J. (1998). Twice upon a time. *The Canadian Journal of Environmental Education, 3,* 116–135.

Shure, M., & Spivak, G. (1978). *Problem solving techniques in child rearing.* San Francisco: Jossey-Bass.

Smilansky, S. (1990). Sociodramatic play: Its relevance to behavior and achievement in school. In E. Klugman & S. Smilansky (Eds.), *Children's play and learning: Perspectives and policy implications* (pp. 18–42). New York: Teachers College Press.

Spady, W. G. (1994). *Outcomes-based education: Critical issues and answers.* Arlington, VA: American Association of School Administrators.

Steele, B. (1998). *Draw me a story: An illustrated exploration of drawing-as-language.* Winnipeg, Manitoba, Canada: Peguis.

Sylwester, R. (1995). *A celebration of neurons: An educator's guide to the human brain.* Alexandria, VA: Association for Supervision and Curriculum Development.

Tabors, P. (1997). *One child, two languages: Children learning English as a second language.* Baltimore, MD: Paul Brookes.

Thompson, P., Gledd, J., Woods, R., MacDonald, D., Evans, A., & Toga, A. (2000). Growth patterns in the developing brain detected by using continuum mechanical tensor maps. *Nature, 404*(9), March, 190–192.

Vecchi, V. (2002). *Theater curtain.* Reggio Emilia, Italy: Reggio Children.

Viitaniemi, G., Bateman, N., Milne, K., & Shea, E. (1997). *ESL instruction and assessment strategies handbook grades 1–6: A curriculum support for ESL stages of proficiency* (school board document).

Vygotsky, L. S. (1976). The role of play in development. In J. Bruner, A. Jolly, & S. Sylva (Eds.), *Play: Its role in development and evolution.* New York: Penguin.

Vygotsky, L. S. (1978). *Mind in society: The development of higher psychological processes.* Cambridge, MA: Harvard University Press.

Wesson, K. A. (2001). The "Volvo effect": Questioning standardized tests. *Young Children, 56*(2), 16–18.

Wien, C. A. (1995). *Developmentally appropriate practice in "real life": Stories of teacher practical knowledge.* New York: Teachers College Press.

Wien, C. A. (1997). A Canadian in Reggio Emilia: The 1997 study tour. *Canadian Children, 22*(2), 30–38.

Wien, C. A. (1998). Towards a pedagogy of listening: Impressions of the centre for early childhood education, Loyalist College, Belleville, Ontario. *Canadian Children, 23*(1), 12–19.

Wien, C. A. (2000). A Canadian interpretation of Reggio Emilia: Fraser's provocation. *Canadian Children, 25*(1), 20–27.

Wien, C. A., & Dudley-Marling, C. (1998). Limited vision: The Ontario curriculum and outcomes-based learning. *Canadian Journal of Education, 23*(4), 405–420.

Wien, C. A., & Kirby-Smith, S. (1998). Untiming the curriculum: A case study of removing clocks from the program. *Young Children, 53*(5), 8–13.

Wiggins, G., & McTighe, J. (1998). *Understanding by design*. Alexandria, VA: Association for Supervision and Curriculum.

Index

About the Author

Carol Anne Wien is an associate professor in the Faculty of Education at York University, Toronto, Canada. She is the author of *Developmentally Appropriate Practice in "Real Life"* (1995) and a book of fiction, *Turtle Drum* (1994), as well as numerous articles in early childhood education journals. She sees Canadians and Americans as closely interconnected: while she lives and works in Canada, some members of her family are American, and she has lived in the United States on several occasions. She loves writing, jazz, art, and ethnographic research and wants to support teachers and young children. She has long-term interests in emergent curriculum and constructivist teaching, the Reggio Emilia Approach, and integrating the arts into daily life.